JACK WELC

Abridged from *JACK WELCH and the GE WAY*

Robert Slater

D1040541

McGraw-Hill

New York   Chicago   San Francisco   Lisbon   London
Madrid   Mexico City   Milan   New Delhi   San Juan
Seoul   Singapore   Sydney   Toronto

This book is printed on recycled, acid-free paper containing a minimum of 50% recycled de-inked fiber.

CONTENTS

PART IV

HARNESSING YOUR PEOPLE FOR COMPETITIVE ADVANTAGE

PART V

DRIVE QUALITY THROUGHOUT THE ORGANIZATION

PART VI

THE TOUGHEST BOSS/MOST ADMIRED MANAGER IN AMERICA

PREFACE

I am pleased that McGraw-Hill is publishing this abridged version of *Jack Welch and the GE Way*, and I'm delighted that the original edition has enjoyed such wide success since McGraw-Hill first published it in 1998. I have always attributed the book's success to the intense interest in the business community in Jack Welch, the man routinely called the greatest business leader of our era.

When I have had a chance to talk with readers of the book, they have suggested that their great admiration for Jack Welch has to do with two aspects of his business leadership. The first aspect was his pioneering of some of the most critical business strategies of the late twentieth century, among which were restructuring, downsizing, and a focus on being number one or number two in the marketplace. The second was his deep-seated conviction that business is, underneath it all, very simple, and executives should not overcomplicate the whole subject. Now, five and a half years after the publication of *Jack Welch and the GE Way*, Welch's revolutionary approach to business practices and especially his battle cry to make business as uncomplicated as possible resonate once again from the pages of this abridged version.

From the moment that I began to study Jack Welch—in the spring of 1991, after he had been in office for a decade—I sensed that he was a unique figure. Unlike other business leaders, he had crafted a tightly woven, carefully scripted set of business precepts that offered a roadmap for every nook and cranny of business life. I know of no other business leader who has shown what was relevant and irrelevant for maximizing performance with such astounding lucidity and frankness. Perhaps Welch's greatest strength has been his willingness to make unpopular decisions, convinced as he was that he was acting for the general good of his business.

When Jack Welch began his stewardship of General Electric in April 1981, he confronted a business environment that exalted large bureaucracies and celebrated the command-and-control management system. He was horrified. To him, bureaucracies did little more than paralyze decision making, while command-and-control systems only encouraged managers to overmanage.

The Welch legacy, as you will read in these pages, has helped countless business leaders to manage less, diminish bureaucracies, and reduce management layers; it has also been a catalyst for granting greater authority to employees and showing greater respect for their ideas.

Jack Welch served as the Chairman and CEO of General Electric from 1981 until the fall of 2001, a 20-year span during which time the company grew into the most valuable enterprise on earth. In 1981, GE's market value was $12 billion, the tenth largest of all American public companies. It was America's market cap leader from 1993 until the summer of 1998, reaching a high of $598 billion and averaging $400 billion or so during Welch's last years as CEO.

Under Welch's leadership, GE became America's greatest business powerhouse. In 1981 GE had annual sales of $25 billion along with earnings of $1.5 billion. In 2000, the last full year before Welch retired, GE's revenues had reached $129.9 billion, its earnings, $12.7 billion. In 2001, the company's revenues reached to $125.9 billion, while earnings rose to $14.1 billion.

In the 12 years that I have been writing about Jack Welch, I never felt an obligation write even a footnote about his personal life. Indeed, my editors always suggested that I downplay Welch's personal life for two reasons: 1) it really wasn't that interesting, and 2) what distinguished Welch were his business strategies, not what he did in his personal life. But after his retirement, it was his personal life exclusively that interested the media.

No aspects of Welch's personal life are discussed in these pages, for good reason: my assumption remains that Welch's many admirers will continue to be interested solely in his business strategies and ideas. Accordingly, this abridged version of *Jack Welch and the GE Way* focuses entirely on those topics.

P A R T

ACT LIKE A LEADER, NOT A MANAGER

Find great ideas, exaggerate them, and spread them like hell around the business with the speed of light.

CHAPTER 1

EMBRACE CHANGE, DON'T FEAR IT

Change was occurring at a much faster pace than business was reacting to it.

TOO MANY MANAGERS fear change.

Too many managers believe that relying on the status quo is the best business strategy—probably because it's the safest. Jack Welch, the tomorrow-driven leader, said it was nonsense to fear change. He loved change, arguing that change keeps everyone alert.

Change is a large part of the reality of the business environment: new competitors, new products. Ignoring that reality will doom a business. Not fearing change, Welch constantly reinvented General Electric.

From his restructuring initiative of the early 1980s to the companywide Internet initiative in 1999, Welch was constantly evolving tools and methods while keeping the goal the same: never-ending growth.

Start each day as if it were your first day on the job, he told his managers.

Make whatever changes are necessary to improve things.

Reexamine your agenda constantly. Rewrite it, if necessary. That keeps you from falling back on old habits.

Make decisions yourselves, he told employees at the factory level. If you're confident that you are right about something, urge change upon your boss.

DON'T BE AFRAID OF CHANGE—AND DON'T LET YOUR BOSS AVOID CHANGE

Jack Welch's very first change at General Electric was revolutionary.

In 1980, the year before he took over the company, it had been doing very well—or so most people thought. It had sales of $25 billion, with profits of $1.5 billion, and was hailed as a model organization in popular management textbooks. Still, the GE chairman was worried that without some major changes in its structure, its products, and its size, GE would falter.

He knew that the business environment was becoming more competitive and sensed that GE had to adjust and adapt as required. Because, as he liked to say, change has no constituency and few in business find change enjoyable, he would have trouble rallying huge numbers of employees behind his plans. Tweaking a tradition-bound company like General Electric seemed absurd to many people.

But not to Jack Welch.

In contrast to almost everyone else, he understood the perils that confronted large corporations like GE during the 1970s and 1980s: high-tech industries and global competitors, who were challenging GE for sales and market share by being more productive and producing higher-quality products. These changes, occurring at an increasingly rapid pace, gave Welch the opportunity to create a new General Electric, more in tune with the evolving business environment. A quick fix would not work; only the most dramatic, far-reaching changes that any major American business enterprise had ever undertaken would succeed. The shouts of junior GE executives arguing that the company was in fine shape did not intimate him. He knew he was right.

He knew for instance that the Asians posed a serious threat:

The Japanese had moved since the late Sixties and early Seventies from poor quality and low prices to low price and high quality. And their plants and their quality and their discipline were overwhelming us in some businesses.

A PROCESS THAT HAD NO NAME

No one had dared to make such monumental changes before. The changes that Welch pioneered in the early 1980s were so new that the process had no name.

Today we call it "restructuring."

Only a handful of General Electric's 350 business units were leaders in their markets:

- Lighting
- Power systems
- Motors

Only three GE products had a reasonably good share of the export market:

- Plastics
- Gas turbines
- Aircraft engines

Of these, only gas turbines enjoyed market leadership overseas. Still, deceptively, GE's balance sheets in the 1970s seemed to glow with health.

Welch knew, however, that American manufacturing was becoming less and less profitable. Yet, as late as 1970 fully 80 percent of General Electric's earnings came from its traditional electrical and electronic manufacturing businesses.

The company had financial achievements, to be sure, especially in plastics, medical systems, and financial services. But these businesses contributed only one-third of GE's total 1981 earnings. In addition, a number of GE's businesses (aircraft engines was the best example) often consumed more cash than they generated.

For decades, the United States had dominated the most important markets of the world economy:

- Steel
- Textiles
- Shipbuilding
- Television
- Calculators
- Automobiles

So, few American business leaders noticed when others, especially the Japanese, began to steal customers by seducing them with higher-quality products bearing cheaper price tags.

Smokestack America was deteriorating. By the summer of 1981, the country was on the brink of recession. To meet competition from around the world, the United States had to become more productive and more aggressive—fast. Yet few American companies were exporting products. Only 1 percent of American companies accounted for 80 percent of the nation's exports.

WHY NOT JUST STAND PAT?

Jack Welch could have gambled that GE, the 115-year-old icon of business, was so strong that it could withstand any economic turbulence. GE executives did not understand why he seemed intent on fixing something that wasn't broken. GE was, after all, generating enormous sales and profits. But Welch knew better:

> I could see a lot of [GE] businesses becoming . . . lethargic. American business was inwardly focused on the bureaucracy, [which] was right for its time, but the times were changing rapidly.

An important building block of Welch's new strategy was this: Weed out certain businesses. Keep only those that dominate their

markets. From now on, a GE business would have to be **first or second** in its market. If the company could not bring flagging businesses up to speed, it would close or sell them.

Hence there arose the famous Welch dictum: **Fix, Close, or Sell!**

That new policy positioned GE for solid growth throughout the 1980s and early 1990s. It was the first of numerous changes that Welch embraced in his two decades as GE Chairman and CEO, reflecting his belief that change was a fruitful, necessary business strategy.

IT'S OK TO ACQUIRE!

GE had in its pre-Welch days advocated that it was better to nurture one's own business than to acquire from outside. In the mid-1980s Welch took a dramatic step, reversing this time-honored tradition.

On December 12, 1985, General Electric purchased RCA, the communications giant, which included the NBC Television Network, the jewel in its crown, for $6.28 billion. At the time General Electric was the ninth largest U.S. industrial firm. RCA was second among the nation's service firms. Together, GE and RCA formed a new corporate power with sales of $40 billion, placing it seventh on the *Fortune* 500. When others called the merger, which aimed at developing GE's highest-growth businesses, countercultural—in other words, a huge change—Welch took it as a compliment.

In June 1987, Welch discarded GE's consumer electronics unit, one of the company's most cherished businesses, in order to acquire a medical diagnostics enterprise. He deemed it "mission impossible" to turn the $3 billion-a-year division, the leading American maker of television sets and video recording equipment, into a first- or second-rank player. He wanted to place the company's resources behind a business that had the potential to become a market leader.

Thus GE turned the division over to Thomson S. A., the largest of the electronics companies. In return, GE acquired the Thomson-CGR medical-imaging unit, which had been selling about $750 million of x-ray and other diagnostic machines in Europe annually. This gave GE entrée into the European medical diagnostic market.

The media attacked Welch ferociously for selling a business that had seemed quintessentially American and for exporting manufacturing jobs.

He scoffed at such criticism: GE had to change; it had to make its businesses market leaders.

Embracing change again in 1989, Welch sensed that his workers were eager for a confidence booster, having witnessed massive layoffs in the 1980s and fearing for their jobs. Until 1989, Welch and his colleagues had doubted there was much to learn from their employees, believing instead that the workers, like drones, were just supposed to carry out management's decisions. But eventually the chairman began to realize that GE's employees were a vital source of new and imaginative ideas. Encouraging their input into day-to-day operations could improve business and dramatically increase productivity. This approach could also make workers who were survivors of past downsizing feel more satisfied in their jobs. Welch launched his Work-Out program, which empowered GE employees to suggest changes in the company's operations, big and small, in order to make GE more efficient. It was the first company to implement such a program on such a large scale.

THE PROOF LIES IN THE PUDDING

Change worked, and Welch knew that it worked because GE's numbers were improving. By the mid-1990s GE had become the strongest company in the nation and the most valuable company in the world, as measured in market capitalization. Even that record of achievement did not keep Welch from searching for further change.

In 1995 he took a bold new step, launching a companywide initiative to improve the quality of General Electric's products and processes. It was bold because it tacitly admitted that GE's products and processes could stand improvement. He had often said that "GE today is a quality company. It has always been a quality company." He could have kept saying that; but instead he vowed:

> **We want to be more than that. We want to change the competitive landscape by being not just better than our competitors, but by taking quality to a whole new level. We want to make our quality so special, so valuable to our customers, so important to their success that our products become their only real value choice.**

Change. It may seem easy to do, but it's not easy to discard old ways. Only through change, though—massive change—could GE win, and Jack Welch firmly believed in winning.

The Jack Welch GE Way Prescription for Change:

➤ *Accept change.* To be a successful business leader, do not treat change like the enemy. Instead, develop a positive attitude toward change. Learn how to read the ever-changing business environment.

➤ *Never stop thinking about how to change.* Encourage your employees to believe that changes, when they happen, can become positive opportunities.

➤ *Review your agenda continuously.* Look for ways to make change in that agenda. Don't assume that the way you are doing things up to now cannot be improved. Ask yourself: What improvements can I make in my agenda today?

CHAPTER 2

STOP MANAGING, START LEADING

Weak managers are the killers of business; they are the job killers.

FOR A LONG TIME, the conventional wisdom in American business was that managers should do little else but keep a watchful eye on their subordinates:

- Monitor
- Supervise
- Control

As a result, junior and senior managers talked only to one another. They shot memos to each other. They held high-level meetings to make sure the company operated smoothly. They were supposed to monitor and control, but not inspire.

They were not supposed to give junior managers the opportunity to be autonomous, entrepreneurial. Nor should they have direct contact with the men and women who actually *produced* the company's wares.

With American corporations seemingly doing fine, who could argue? Jack Welch, for one. He despises such bureaucrats and considers them relics of the past. He believes they overmanage.

Here is a brief **self-assessment exercise** to help you determine whether you are one of those "command-and-control" types that Welch abhors:

1. Do you hold meetings constantly?

       Yes   **No**

2. Do you issue memos continuously?

       Yes   **No**

3. Do you insist on layers of communication and confirmation, such as written approvals?

       Yes   **No**

If you answered all three in the affirmative, then you are needlessly adding bureaucracy—a management practice frowned upon by Welch.

Essentially, Welch asks one key question when it comes to management: Is it better to be hands-on or hands-off? His answer: The *less* managed, the better off the company. He dislikes the very notion of "management." Most managers, in his view, *overmanage* and in so doing help to create the bureaucratic sloth and sluggishness that kills large companies.

From the very moment that he took over as head of General Electric, Welch regarded the place as a bureaucratic dinosaur. Management did too much controlling and monitoring. If he was going to get GE to successfully compete in an increasingly complex and competitive business environment, he would have to discard the concept of manager altogether because it had come to mean someone who "controls rather than facilitates, complicates rather than simplifies, acts more like a governor than an accelerator."

Some managers, Welch said, muddle business decisions with pointless complexity and detail:

> **They equate [managing] with sophistication, with sounding smarter than anyone else. They inspire no one. I dislike the traits that have come to be associated with "managing"—controlling, stifling people, keeping them in the dark, wasting their time on trivia and reports. Breathing down their necks.**

He preferred the term *leader*. Leaders "inspire with clear vision of how things can be done better."

MANAGERS MUDDLE–LEADERS INSPIRE

Managers slow things down. Leaders spark the business to run smoothly and quickly. Managers talk to one another, write memos to one another. Leaders talk to their employees, talk *with* their employees, filling them with vision, getting them to perform at levels the employees themselves didn't think possible. Then—and to Welch this is a critical ingredient—they simply get out of the way.

Above all else, Welch wanted his business leaders to keep things simple.

Managing need not be overly complicated, he stressed, because business is actually quite uncomplicated:

> **We've chosen one of the world's most simple professions. Most global businesses have three or four critical competitors, and you know who they are. And there aren't that many things you can do with a business. It's not as if you're choosing among two thousand options.**

To Welch, the secret of running a successful business is to make sure that all key decision makers in that business have access to the same set of facts. If they have, they will all reach roughly the same conclusion about how to handle a business issue. The problem, he said, is that they *don't* get the same information; rather, they get different pieces of information.

ASK THE RIGHT QUESTIONS

To Welch, the business leader who is good at keeping things simple knows just what questions to ask of his subordinates:

1. *What does your global competitive environment look like?*
2. *In the last three years, what have your competitors done?*

3. *In that same period, what have you done?*
4. *How might competitors attack you in the future?*
5. *What are your plans to leapfrog over them?*

That's all managing is, said the chairman and CEO of General Electric: just coming up with the right questions and getting the right answers.

SUPERLEADER

Running the mighty General Electric enterprise, with its numerous major businesses, Jack Welch did not seem like a manager in the normal sense of the word. He seemed more like a superleader.

What is the main task of a superleader who supervises an array of major businesses?

> **My job is to put the best people on the biggest opportunities and the best allocation of dollars in the right places. That's about it.**

Transfer ideas and allocate resources and get out of the way.

He did not get involved in, say, deciding on the style of a refrigerator. He left that to the experts:

> **I have no idea how to produce a good [television] program and just as little about how to build an engine . . . But I do know who the boss at NBC is. It is my job to choose the best people and to provide them with the dollars.**

To Welch, having the right kind of managers in place was essential for success. A strong leader can shock an organization and lead its recovery. An ineffectual leader will shock an organization—and paralyze, even kill it:

> **My job is to find great ideas, exaggerate them, and spread them like hell around the business with the speed of light . . . And to put resources in to support them. Keep finding ideas. That's the job of just about all of our CEOs.**

He was emphatic that a true leader doesn't *run* a business: "I don't *run* GE. I *lead* GE." He could not micromanage such multibillion-dollar corporations as GE Capital and NBC.

What kind of goals did Welch set for his business leaders?

> **I don't set them. In the old days, they'd set a goal and I'd set one and then we'd negotiate. Now, we don't reward them according to whether or not they reach their objectives. In bureaucratic companies, they waste a lot of time on making budgets. They waste energy. The world is changing quickly. We can't afford to waste time in bureaucracy.**

Being a business leader in the late 1990s became far more demanding, Welch asserts, than in earlier years:

> **Today form isn't allowed. Global battles don't allow form. It's all substance. Form means somebody is not intensely interested in the company. Somebody on umpteen boards. Somebody off giving speeches all the time. Somebody that doesn't have their eye on the ball. Somebody who has reached the position of chairman as the culmination of a career, rather than the beginning of a career. See, my career starts again next January. What I did until now is meaningless. Meaningless. It's just the beginning.**

The Jack Welch GE Way Prescription for Leading:

➤ *Managing less is better.* No one is saying don't manage at all. Just don't get bogged down in overmanaging. That will give you time to think big thoughts and conceive new ideas.

➤ *Manage by creating a vision*—and then make sure that your employees run with that vision.

➤ *Lead, don't manage.* Then get out of the way. Let employees do their jobs without constant interference.

➤ *Instill confidence.* Treat employees with respect in order to build their confidence in your leadership.

CHAPTER 3

CULTIVATE MANAGERS
WHO SHARE YOUR VISION

*What we are looking for . . . are
leaders . . . who can energize, excite,
and control rather than enervate,
depress, and control.*

IF JACK WELCH had little use for autocratic managers who overmanage, overmonitor, and oversupervise, just what kind of managers did he actually like?

First off, they should be bursting with energy. Second, they should be able to actually develop and implement a vision—not just talk incessantly about it. And they must know how to spread enthusiasm like wildfire by firing up the entire company.

The way to engender enthusiasm, said Welch, was to allow employees far more freedom and far more responsibility.

In 1987 he requested a meeting with the head of a particular GE business that had produced profits yet, in the CEO's view, could do better. But Welch's message was lost on the manager. He wanted the manager to develop a vision, to become enthusiastic about his work; to re-energize his employees. He urged the perplexed manager to take a month off and upon his return, do everything differently. The man just didn't comprehend that Welch wanted him to rewrite his agenda, take a new look at the business plan, and see things with a fresh eye. Six months later that executive no longer worked for GE.

GET ON BOARD

As far as Welch was concerned, middle managers had to be team members and coaches; energizers, not enervators. He noted that General Electric once rewarded managers who produced good numbers even if they did not share ideas with people in other aspects of their business. Eventually Welch decided to replace such high-number managers with people who were not as perfect but were good team players.

> **Maybe the predecessor was working at 100 percent or 120 percent, but that person didn't talk with team members, didn't swap ideas. As a result, the whole team was operating at 65 percent. But the new manager is getting 90 percent or 100 percent from the whole total. That was a discovery.**

The Heisman Trophy candidate who wouldn't block for others, a favorite Welch example, had a debilitating effect on a team.

> **To be blunt, the two quickest ways to part company with GE are, one, to commit an integrity violation, or, two, to be a controlling, turf-defending, oppressive manager who can't change and who saps and squeezes people rather than excites and draws out their energy and creativity.**

MY TYPE OF MANAGER

In describing the four types of GE managers and assessing which ones will ultimately succeed—and which ones won't—Jack Welch was essentially suggesting that the *only* way to last at General Electric was to become a team player by adapting oneself to the company's values and culture.

The first type delivers on commitments—financial or otherwise—and shares GE's values. Welch liked such leaders and would make sure they stuck around.

The second type did not meet commitments (read "bring in a healthy balance sheet") and did not share GE's values. Out the door they went.

The third type missed commitments but shared values. Welch was sympathetic, and such managers usually got a second chance, preferably in a different environment.

The fourth type delivered on commitments but did not subscribe to GE's values. The fate of such people created the greatest quandary for the chairman.

Eventually, Welch talked less of these four kinds of managers and more of managers who would or would not do well at GE. While there was no one definition, the fate of each type was clear: type A (the team player who subscribed to company values) was to be kept and promoted; type B was to be nurtured in the hope that he or she might improve; and type C (the manager who did not buy into the company's value system) was to be fired.

> **Too many of you work too hard to make C's [into] B's. It is a wheel-spinning exercise. Push C's on to B companies or C companies, and they'll do just fine . . . We're an A-plus company. We want only A players. We can get anyone we want. Take care of your best. Reward them. Promote them. Pay them well. Give them a lot of [stock] options**

When a GE manager once apologetically told Welch that she had recently been forced to let go of a few people, he urged her not to feel guilty or sorry.

Here is a brief **self-assessment exercise** that should help you determine whether you are capable of finding and nurturing the right employees.

1. Do you spend quality time evaluating people?

      Yes   No

2. Do you minimize your human resources efforts?

      Yes   No

3. Do you offer a rewards incentive program that encourages those whom you will one day want to promote?

       Yes   **No**

If you answered 1 and 3 yes, that's a good start toward the goal of finding the best possible employees.

What counsel did Welch give to junior executives to help them become future great leaders?

> **The biggest advice I give people is you cannot do these jobs alone. You've got to be very comfortable with the brightest human beings alive on your team. Always get the best people. If you haven't got one who's good, you're shortchanging yourself.**

But isn't it hard to convince young people who want to make a name for themselves that the main thing is to become a team player? Very hard, Welch acknowledged. That was why he always insisted on managers with the self-confidence and the comfort level to hire brilliant people.

Finding the right employees has become a tough assignment for CEOs.

The business environment of the late 1990s, Welch believed, required an energized, energizing CEO. It was not a job for the faint of heart. Twenty years ago, being named chairman and CEO was the culmination of a career; by the late 1990s, for the CEO who wanted to keep that top job, it was merely the beginning:

> **No one can come to work and sit, no one can go off and think of just policy. You've got to be able to energize others. You cannot be this thoughtful, in-the-corner-of-fice guru. You cannot be a moderate, balanced, thoughtful, careful articulator of policy. You've got to be on the lunatic fringe.**

Welch understood that the nurturing of his managerial talent was one of the main keys to GE's success. He paid special attention to shifting around that talent, particularly at the higher levels. His involvement in these hiring decisions was testament to the importance Welch placed on decisions affecting people.

The Jack Welch GE Way Prescription for Nurturing Leaders:

➤ Find leaders who are willing to swallow their egos, blur their identities, and work for the overall good of the company.

➤ Offer employees more responsibility and they will make better decisions.

➤ Make employees more accountable and the organization will become more productive.

➤ Nurture those employees who adhere to company values even if they don't make their numbers.

➤ Re-assign employees who live up to company values but don't make the numbers. Eliminate those who fail to follow company values even if they make their numbers.

CHAPTER 4

FACE REALITY, THEN ACT DECISIVELY

In the twenty-first century would you rather be in toasters or CAT scanners?

FACE REALITY. Face the facts and don't flinch.

For Jack Welch, facing reality was critical to business success: Those who are able to acknowledge truth are usually successful. Yet for all sorts of reasons, it is difficult for business leaders to do this. The truth hurts. The truth is embarrassing.

Still, the art of leading comes down to facing reality—about situations, products, and people—and then acting quickly and decisively on that reality. Most mistakes that business leaders make, says Welch, arise from being unwilling to face reality and act accordingly.

Hard realities must be faced, in Welch's view:

- The world is becoming increasingly competitive.
- No job is guaranteed for life.
- Managing a business by erecting huge bureaucracies is ineffective.
- Business is really simple.

In October 1981, six months after he became chairman and CEO, Welch spelled out his revolutionary plans for a new GE to 120 company officers: There would be no more bureaucratic waste, no more deceptive budgets and plans. No one would be able to hide from tough decisions.

In short, from then on, General Electric's employees were going to stare reality in the face—and acknowledge it.

BETTER TO BE IN TOASTERS OR IN CAT SCANNERS?

The first reality Welch observed was the rising peril of foreign competition. He was alone in discerning that peril.

To combat increasing competitiveness from abroad, it would be critical, he believed, to restructure the company radically by reducing the size of GE's workforce and jettisoning underperforming businesses.

Scrapping GE's housewares business in 1983 was an early example of Jack Welch facing reality. For General Electric employees, giving up on toasters and irons and fans was like selling off the company's heritage. These products had made the company a household name. Welch's response was straightforward: "In the twenty-first century, would you rather be in toasters or in CAT scanners?"

By the early 1980s, GE's strengths were lost in a business like housewares, where as soon as the company produced a great new hair dryer, for example, a lower-priced knockoff appeared. Its strengths were in technological and financial resources that enabled it to invest hundreds of millions of dollars and the required time to develop a new generation of jet engines, gas turbines, a new-generation plastic, or a new-generation medical diagnostic imaging machine.

Welch stared reality in the face in 1986 when GE merged with RCA, developing for General Electric a serious, service-oriented dimension that would boost its success.

He faced a new reality in the late 1980s: that every truth or facet of wisdom about how to run a business did not reside with GE's senior management. Welch acknowledged that the factory workers and junior executives—those closest to GE's products and customers—had as good a sense of GE's operations as senior management, maybe better. He thus began the companywide Work-Out program that raised workers' morale by giving them a sense of ownership in the company and contributed to GE's productivity by capturing and implementing ideas from junior personnel for the first time.

By the mid-1990s, Welch faced yet another reality relating to quality. For years Welch, convinced that GE's products and processes were of a superior quality to its competitors, was not a great believer in programs designed to further enhance that quality. But GE employees urged Welch to face reality and realize that in fact much needed to be done to improve GE products and processes. Welch responded in 1995, and GE began a quality initiative based on the increasingly popular six sigma approach. Six sigma is a measurement of mistakes per one million discreet operations. It applies to all transactions, not just manufacturing. The fewer the errors, the higher the quality.

In the late 1990s, Welch faced yet another reality—about the company as a whole. Welch's goal for GE never wavered; it was always ever-increasing growth. Yet he was aware that the manufacturing side was not going to deliver the double-digit growth that he demanded. Accordingly, he mounted a new campaign to increase GE's role in providing service.

IN ALL CANDOR

Facing reality also meant being candid, in Welch's view, so on occasion he admitted to making mistakes. For instance, he regretted not buying a food company in the early days. His biggest mistake of all, he felt, was not moving more quickly to implement major changes at GE.

I would have liked to have done things a lot faster. I've been here for seventeen years. Imagine if I'd taken four,

**three, or even one year too long in making my decisions. I
would have had a rude awakening. I would very much
have liked, for example, to get all my divisions working together ten years ago.**

In Welch's case, such admissions came easy if only because he
had been so successful. His track record spoke for itself. But other
business leaders need encouragement at facing reality.

The Jack Welch GE Way Prescription for Facing Reality:

➤ *Face the facts and don't flinch.* Failure comes to business
leaders who avoid reality.

➤ *Act on reality with all due speed.* Adapt your business
strategies to adapt to the new reality quickly.

➤ *Don't assume that just because the business seems to be
doing well that you have learned to face reality.* Always
face into the prospect that there is a new reality around
the corner that you need to recognize.

CHAPTER 5

BE SIMPLE, BE CONSISTENT, AND HAMMER YOUR MESSAGE HOME

The only way to change people's minds is with consistency.

*R*ELENTLESS CONSISTENCY.

Jack Welch is almost fanatic when it comes to relentless consistency. He believes in applying the business tenet to everything: checking a factory's plans, determining whether training programs are effective, making sure that company values are alive and well at every level of the organization. Put another way: *Follow up on everything. It is a key measure of success for a business.*

GE's chairman had little use for managers who called meetings and set goals but never followed up to see if those goals were achieved:

> **Somebody runs the January meeting and they leave and say, "Nice going," and they thank the person that ran it. "It was a great meeting." Then they have a March meeting. Somebody else runs that. And he brings in somebody else. Then they have a long-range planning session, and there's no relationship to the meeting they ran in January.**

A FEW THEMES, A FEW PHRASES

Follow-up to Welch also meant harping on a few key themes and repeating them incessantly. In the early days of the Welch era, the key themes were:

- Number one, number two
- Fix, close, or sell
- Speed, simplicity, and self-confidence

In the late 1990s, the key phrases were:

- Boundarylessness
- Work-Out
- Stretch
- Quality
- Service
- Learning Culture

The GE Values Guide

The key words and phrases popped up in all sorts of places—in Jack Welch's annual Letter to Share Owners, in his speeches to the GE board, in talks with financial analysts, and on a small, wallet-size card that GE employees carried with them. Before the cards were furnished to the staff, GE had to come to some consensus on which core values it wanted to cultivate in its employees.

What were the GE values inscribed on that wallet-size card? GE Leaders . . . Always with Unyielding Integrity:

- Have a Passion for Excellence and Hate Bureaucracy
- Are Open to Ideas from Anywhere . . . and Committed to Work-Out
- Live Quality . . . and Drive Cost and Speed for Competitive Advantage

- Have the Self-Confidence to Involve Everyone and Behave in a Boundaryless Fashion
- Create a Clear, Simple, Reality-Based Vision . . . and Communicate It to All Constituencies
- Have Enormous Energy and the Ability to Energize Others
- Stretch . . . Set Aggressive Goals . . . Reward Progress . . . Yet Understand Accountability and Commitment
- See Change as Opportunity . . . Not Threat
- Have Global Brains . . . and Build Diverse and Global Teams

BE CONSISTENT—CONSISTENTLY!

Being relentlessly consistent and following up means making sure that the identical no-nonsense message gets delivered to every audience, whether it's the GE board, financial analysts, labor unions, or GE employees. Welch credited the follow-up business strategy with paving the way for GE's success:

> **It's not that I changed. You don't get anywhere if you keep changing your ideas. The only way to change people's minds is with consistency. If you have a simple, consistent message, and you keep on repeating it, eventually that's what happens.**

Here is a brief **self-assessment exercise** to help you determine whether you are issuing consistent messages to those below you:

1. Do you emphasize certain themes of the business to one audience but not another?

    Yes   No

2. Do you articulate one set of messages one year and another set the next year?

    Yes   No

3. Do you leave follow-up to others?

    Yes   No

If you answered these three questions in the negative, you need to do much more to become relentlessly consistent.

Welch's consistency had indeed helped to revive GE and remake it into one of the world's most competitive companies. It certainly didn't hurt that so much of what he predicted about the business world actually came true. As his legend grew with every correct prediction, so did the respect of the GE workforce.

However, as Welch recalled, the journey was often arduous and at times downright painful. Welch noted how difficult it was for GE employees to swallow what he calls his "change ideas." But he took great pride in the fact that so many of his calls had been correct—that the world had become more global, more service-oriented, and far more competitive. And as he pounded his message home over the years, he won the hearts and minds of the GE workforce and converted critics into believers. By accomplishing this, he created a far more fertile environment for change—and that made his task of transforming GE that much easier.

The Jack Welch GE Way Prescription for Relentless Consistency:

➤ Present consistent messages about your business over the long haul.

➤ Present consistent themes and strategies to every audience you address.

➤ Articulate your messages, and then engage in a follow-up campaign to assure those messages are getting through.

BUILDING THE MARKET-LEADING COMPANY

What can I do to make one of my businesses dominant in its market?

CHAPTER 6

BE NUMBER ONE OR NUMBER TWO, BUT DON'T NARROW YOUR MARKET

When you're number four or five in a market, you get pneumonia when number one sneezes.

IN BUSINESS, Jack Welch asserted, the strong survive, the weak do not. The big and fast get to play, the small and slow are left behind.

Success rewards those who become more competitive. And market leaders have an easier time becoming competitive.

To gain competitive advantage, Welch developed a strategy that required all GE businesses to be either first or second in their fields. By exacting the highest standards, he hoped to avoid creating and nurturing mediocre players who, he was sure, would eventually lose out:

> **I saw businesses that were number five in the marketplace, not even number three, that we were holding onto as a shrine to our past. I always felt sorry for the people in the bad ones because they never saw a good one. They always compared themselves with their direct competitor. So if their returns were nine and their competitor's seven, they were doing very well.**

Welch evolved a game plan, a business strategy he called "number one, number two." He was convinced that inflation would become the most prominent enemy confronting American business in the 1980s, leading to slower worldwide growth. That meant there would be no room for the mediocre supplier of products and services. His argument:

> **The winners would be those who insisted upon being the number one or number two leanest, lowest-cost, worldwide producers of quality goods and services or those who had a clear technological edge or a clear advantage in their chosen niche.**

WHY PICK ON US? WHAT HAVE WE DONE WRONG?

It was clear to Welch that being number one in the market was far easier and better than being in weaker businesses. The weaker businesses lacked the resources, muscle, and power to compete on a global scale. If General Electric found itself in a business that was not number one or number two in its field, and that did not have a technological edge, the tough question had to be asked: "If you weren't already in this business, would you enter it today?"

If the answer was no, then swift action had to be taken. Welch predicted that corporations in the 1980s that hung on to losers, whether out of tradition or sentiment or their own management weakness, would not be around by 1990.

GE's business leaders were expected to ask which businesses were worth nurturing and which were not. In the early 1980s, GE had quite a number of profitable businesses that were third or fourth in their fields. Leaders of those businesses didn't understand why they had to be dismantled. The new chairman felt he had no choice, no matter how painful those decisions were:

> **When you're number four or five in a market, when number one sneezes, you get pneumonia. When you're number one, you control your destiny. The number fours keep merging; they have difficult times.**

No Untidy Conglomerate

To Welch and others, GE appeared to lack a central focus. It was not only large, it was diverse. Welch presided over an extensive and varied portfolio of businesses—350 in all, clustered in forty-three strategic business units. Few other American enterprises were so intricate. In the early 1980s it was producing nuclear reactors and microwave ovens, robots and silicon chips; it had businesses in time-sharing services and Australian coking coal. While that diversity had given General Electric earnings protection from economic downturns, investors had trouble understanding what GE produced—and how it would perform in the future.

Welch wanted to send the message to Wall Street that General Electric was not some untidy conglomerate with all kinds of scattered and unrelated businesses. The company had a purpose and a focus. It was determined to become the most competitive enterprise on earth. And it would reach that goal by making sure all of its businesses were first or second in their markets.

Welch took a pad and pencil and sketched three circles. One circle contained GE's core businesses; the second circle contained GE's high-technology businesses; and the third circle contained its service businesses. Those businesses inside the circle Welch wanted to nourish; those outside, he wanted to jettison unless they could be fixed. He adopted the motto: Fix, close, or sell.

HOW CAN I GET INTO THAT CIRCLE?

Fifteen businesses, which when taken in aggregate produced 90 percent of 1984 corporate earnings, were in the circles.

The three-circle concept, Jack Welch's compass during the early 1980s, was designed to instill clarity into an organization that outsiders had described as a confusing conglomerate. Here's how the three circles broke down:

1. *Core Circle:* Lighting, Major Appliance, Motor, Transportation, Turbine, Contractor Equipment

2. *Technology Circle:* Industrial Electronics, Medical Systems, Materials, Aerospace, Aircraft Engines
3. *Services Circle:* General Electric Credit Corporation, Information, Construction, and Engineering, Nuclear Services

Outside the circle were these GE businesses: Housewares, Central Air Conditioning, TV and Audio, Cable, Mobile Communications, Power Delivery, Radio Stations, Ladd Petroleum, Semiconductor, Trading, Utah International, and Calma.

One-fifth of General Electric's businesses, valued at $9 billion, did not make the grade. GE let go of 117 businesses and product sectors, including coal mines, semiconductors, toasters, hair dryers, and clocks. Meanwhile, GE purchased assets that totaled $16 billion.

Winning was what mattered to Welch, not tradition. During a one-year period he got rid of both Housewares and Utah International, a mining subsidiary that former CEO Reg Jones had bought only eight years earlier. In another twelve-month period Welch bought RCA, which included NBC, the television network, and Kidder Peabody, an investment bank.

I HATE THAT NAME!

Welch's early restructuring efforts won the new chairman sharp criticism. He was often described in the media as "Neutron Jack," an allusion to the neutron bomb that eliminates people but leaves buildings standing. He hated the name because it suggested that he had been unfair to his employees, that he had pushed them into the streets without a way to make a living.

> **I have never laid off anyone. Even when selling businesses, I have set aside twice as much as retirement money for employees and have given them as good a safety net as possible before they have left.**

By the late 1980s, Welch's number one, number two strategy had evolved. Now, the chairman wanted his businesses to dominate not simply the American market but the world market as well.

Ironically, when it came to the business that would eventually become GE's most important revenue driver, GE Capital, the number one, number two strategy really didn't apply. The financial service business was too broad. Citibank was the largest and had only 1 percent of the market.

A FLAW IN THE STRATEGY

While the strategy worked for General Electric during the 1980s, by the mid-1990s GE discovered a built-in flaw: Over time, the strategy tended to be limited. After a while, the natural tendency of GE managers in search of market dominance was to define their markets in a way that virtually guaranteed that they were number one or number two. Thus, they wound up defining those markets narrowly when it was far better for them to define them broadly.

One example was GE's power generation business, which produced products for the big utilities. In focusing its energies on huge power plants—and defining the market as consisting of such—GE neglected the smaller but burgeoning distributed-power market that had developed all over the world. GE wasn't making products in that area at all, because when it defined its market that segment was conveniently identified as being outside of GE's purview. When customers required smaller units, the power generation business simply decided such products were not worth manufacturing.

In late 1995, Welch was urged by members of a business management course at GE's Crotonville site to refine his strategy so that GE businesses would not define their markets as being any more narrow than 10 percent of the total market. The mandate of GE's businesses would be to pursue a larger portion of the newly defined market. Welch liked what he heard. The recommendation was implemented in early 1996.

This refinement dovetailed nicely with GE's plans to infuse more of a service dimension into its businesses. While historically GE had provided service and parts for GE engines only, in 1997 it began offering repair and parts for GE, Pratt & Whitney, and Rolls Royce aircraft engines. In short, GE was defining the aircraft engine market far more broadly in order to capture more service-oriented business.

Could redefining markets make it harder for GE to remain in its number one or two position? GE executives did not think so. They were confident that GE would figure out how to remain on top by working more aggressively to capture a larger share of the newly defined market.

The Jack Welch GE Way Prescription for Assuring Market Leadership:

➤ Examine every business you are in and determine which are underperforming and which are not. Jettison the underperformers.

➤ If a business is a marginal underperformer, decide whether it is worth fixing. If it is, work hard at getting it to a point where it can lead the market at number one or two.

➤ Be careful, in seeking market leadership, that you do not define your market too narrowly. That can lead you to the deceptive situation where you are a market leader but are depriving your company of going after more business.

CHAPTER 7

LOOK FOR THE QUANTUM LEAP!

*I don't think I've moved fast enough
or incisively enough.*

*J*ACK WELCH BELIEVED IN THE SURPRISE MOVE. The bold play. He loved the idea that he could shake things up while others looked on from the sidelines, sitting idly by while he knocked his competitors for a loop.

Surprise. Boldness. Shock. These were the crucial, critical ingredients of the quantum leap: Welch's conquest of RCA.

Because for most of its history GE had grown from within, acquiring RCA was a revolutionary move for the company. It simply had not believed in growing by acquisition. But Jack Welch believed that to adhere to outdated traditions was to avoid reality. Although he was concerned about criticism that GE was just one more renegade conglomerate that bought and sold businesses by the seat of its pants, he remained confident that he could acquire and divest and still remain focused.

By 1985, Jack Welch's revolution was well in stride. Annual sales at GE had increased from $27.24 billion in 1981 to $28.29 billion in 1985, and GE was the tenth largest of the *Fortune* 500 companies, up a notch from the year before. Even more important, its earnings had risen 2 percent in 1985, to $2.33 billion, which made GE the fifth most profitable company in the United States. Contributing immeasurably to those improved earnings was the $5.6 billion worth of businesses that Welch had sold since taking over as CEO.

Welch made it clear that he was not averse to grabbing a large company if the fit and price were right. He cast his eyes on the Radio Corporation of America, one of America's most famous corporate names. In 1984, RCA's sales had topped $10 billion.

STRIKING A DEAL FOR THE PEACOCK

To Welch the RCA acquisition made perfect sense. After all, he needed a cash flow stream that would compensate for his manufacturing businesses, which were coming under increasing pressure. He viewed service businesses as the solution to any possible future cash flow problems.

At NBC, part of RCA, the reaction to having GE as a new parent was mixed at best. NBC News executives were concerned that General Electric would interfere with the news operation. Welch assured them that would not be the case.

AND WHAT ABOUT NIPPER?

The NBC television network, which had faltered some years earlier, was on an upswing in the mid-1980s, making it more attractive to Welch.

Grant Tinker, the head of NBC, had performed miracles in the early 1980s, improving the network's ratings with a series of highly popular shows, including *Hill Street Blues, Cheers, St. Elsewhere,* and *Family Ties.*

It had other hits such as *Golden Girls, Alf, Matlock, L. A. Law,* and *Amen.* Its biggest hit was *The Cosby Show,* which sometimes won its time slot with a whopping 50 percent share of the market.

In 1984, the network's earnings of $248 million formed fully 43 percent of RCA's $567 million total; a year later, the network's earnings had risen to $376 million. NBC was truly the jewel in RCA's crown.

Though the purchase was certainly the largest counterculture step GE had ever taken, purchasing the communications giant for $6.28 billion (or $66.50 a share) seemed a very good deal. Some analysts felt RCA was worth $90 a share.

CURBING THE BIG SPENDERS

Now that he had made his quantum leap, the GE chairman wanted to impose the GE culture on the new acquisition. It was a real test: GE had its own business culture, and so did NBC.

Welch wanted NBC to face the reality that times were tough. The free-spending network could no longer function without budgetary constraints. He would not permit this to be his Waterloo.

For years the three major television networks had functioned without having to be concerned about costs. But when Welch came along in the mid-1980s he expected the same response from NBC as from his aircraft engines or lighting business:

- To be profitable
- To be careful with expenses
- To fit into the General Electric culture

Unhappy network staffers were not eager to face reality. They feared that the venerable Peacock Network, famous for Milton Berle, Huntley-Brinkley, and *Bonanza,* would simply become another cog in the GE machine. And one early GE decision seemed to confirm their greatest fears: Welch announced that he was changing the name of the landmark RCA Building at 30 Rockefeller Center to the GE Building. NBC employees were appalled.

Welch had a hard time fathoming how the network that had the highest ratings also had the lowest profits. And he could not understand how NBC could justify its huge budget. The NBC News budget alone had mushroomed from $207.3 million in 1983 to $282.5 million in 1984. And because advertising on NBC's news program never equaled the news division's expenses, NBC News lost millions of dollars. In 1988, the year Michael Gartner was hired to replace Lawrence K. Grossman as NBC News president, the operation lost $126 million.

Welch had truly been stymied by Larry Grossman's attitude. When Grossman said to him that because the network was a public trust, NBC News should not have to confront the type of bottom-line pressures that other GE business units had to endure, Welch went ballistic.

He believed that he, too, had a public trust: It had to do with making sure that refrigerators did not explode and airplanes did not crash. Welch's customers put their lives in his hands. In short, NBC did not deserve an exemption from GE's "face reality" credo.

Welch turned the network around quickly. In 1985, NBC had profits of $333 million. The following year profits rose to $350 million, while revenues soared past the $3 billion mark for the first time, buoyed by the network's first-place ratings. The *Today* show was ranked first, as was *NBC Nightly News with Tom Brokaw.* The network's financial picture brightened further in the late 1980s, and its profits ballooned to $750 million in 1989.

As NBC moved into the 1990s, the competitive pressures increased, and the network found it difficult to maintain the huge audiences and the heady profits of the preceding decade.

I've Moved Too Slowly

After several years at number one, NBC slipped to third place by the end of 1992. Its profits slipped down to $204 million in 1992. And while GE had encouraged its business leaders to hire the strongest person possible for each job, NBC president Robert Wright had chosen Michael Gartner, a respected newspaper editor, as president of NBC News. Gartner had an unhappy ride at NBC. Though he managed to curb losses in the news division by cutting costs, critics blamed him for a variety of inept behavior—from bungling the *Today* show's transition from co-anchor Jane Pauley to Deborah Norville to offering the tabloid TV show, *I Witness Video.*

On the entertainment side, when Brandon Tartikoff left NBC to run Paramount in 1991, Wright turned prime time over to Tartikoff's deputy, Warren Littlefield, a great programmer with limited business skills. Also that year, after a much-heralded negotiation that inspired a book and an HBO movie, popular talk-show host David Letterman jumped ship to CBS.

But Jack Welch had completed his quantum leap. He had a new business strikingly different from the traditional GE businesses of yesteryear—lighting, power generation, major appliances. It was much easier to bring these manufacturing divisions into line with GE's emerging corporate culture, but far more difficult to tame the folks at NBC. None of this diminished the value of making the bold ploy, however, of surprising competitors and grabbing the initiative. And that's precisely what Welch had achieved in acquiring NBC.

The Jack Welch GE Way Prescription for Making a Quantum Leap:

➤ When planning to grow your company, think big, think outside the box. Don't assume that you can successfully expand simply by relying upon your own employees and managers.

➤ Think about making outside acquisitions, but examine all prospects with great care and strike at just the right time. When you're sure that you're making the right move, act quickly. Hesitating can cost you the deal.

➤ Act with both boldness and stealth in order to catch your rivals off guard. Don't let on that you are seeking to acquire another company until the last possible minute.

CHAPTER 8

FIX, CLOSE, OR SELL:
REVIVING NBC

*Getting great talent, giving them all the
support in the world, and letting them
run is the whole management
philosophy of GE.*

*T*HE EARLY 1990s had been difficult years for NBC, and there
was constant buzz that Jack Welch would sell the network. Most of
those who prophesied an eventual NBC sale failed to take into
account one of Welch's key business strategies: fix, close, or sell.

Welch had a special affection for the network. There was, after
all, a lot more glamour in owning NBC—home of *Seinfeld, ER,* and
The Tonight Show—than in owning a light bulb business. Coaxed
along by NBC president Bob Wright, who had great faith in his
own ability to turn the network around, Welch decided to "fix"
NBC with a series of quick, clever maneuvers.

Having lost patience with their own division heads in the early
1990s, Welch and Wright decided that NBC needed to replace cur-
rent managers with more business-minded, entrepreneurial leaders. To head entertainment, they chose Don Ohlmeyer; for news,
they chose Andy Lack; and for sports, Dick Ebersol.

PUTTING THE NBC FIX-IT TEAM TOGETHER

Early in 1993, Bob Wright turned to Don Ohlmeyer, a sports and entertainment producer who had run his own production company, hiring him to take over as president of NBC West Coast. Ohlmeyer demanded full control over entertainment along with more freedom to spend money on programming. Wright concurred.

Ohlmeyer produced the best results of all the aggressive managers Wright had appointed, carrying out one of Welch's favorite business strategies. By holding a daily 2:30 P.M. "war room" meeting of department heads for brainstorming, Ohlmeyer tore down internal barriers in the division.

Under Ohlmeyer, NBC devised new promotion stunts that worked wonders. Its "Must-See TV" became part of the lexicon. NBC was the first network to eliminate commercial breaks between programs; this kept viewers who had tuned in to one show tuned to the next as well. After a rocky start, *The Tonight Show with Jay Leno* overtook CBS's *Late Show with David Letterman.*

Ohlmeyer provided three years of steady ratings growth in prime-time television programming and attracted the youthful demographics that sponsors wanted. Within eighteen months of his arrival at NBC, megahits *Frasier, Friends,* and *ER* were launched.

His record at NBC was sensational, including the fifteen Emmys he won for his work. He moved NBC Entertainment from number three to number one in the ratings; annual network profits increased from $264 million in 1993 to $738 million in 1995.

Ohlmeyer was not at all inhibited about saying what was on his mind. He compared Rupert Murdoch with Hitler, and labeled Michael Ovitz the Antichrist. He described major league baseball owners as "brain-damaged." Welch was largely forgiving of Ohlmeyer. "There's a lot of Don in every one of us," said Welch. "Most of us don't have the guts to be Don. Our suits constrain us."

Robert Wright hired Andy Lack, an innovative CBS news producer, to run NBC News. Lack, like Don Ohlmeyer, had that entrepreneurial spirit. The *Today* show began to dominate the morning show ratings. *Dateline* grew into a commercial, though not a critical, success. And the *Nightly News with Tom Brokaw* mounted the first serious challenge since the late 1980s to ABC's *World News Tonight,* anchored by Peter Jennings.

Pursuing the Olympics

To run NBC Sports, Wright hired Dick Ebersol. Both Ebersol and Ohlmeyer had worked for Roone Arledge at ABC Sports. Ebersol had produced *Saturday Night Live,* a professional wrestling show, and Bob Costa's late-night NBC talk show. Adapting one of Jack Welch's favorite managerial precepts, Bob Wright in effect was creating the vision and letting his three top executives run with it, all the while demanding that they move fast—another Welch strategy.

The Welch strategy of stressing speed was in evidence when Bob Wright summoned Dick Ebersol and Randy Falco, who were responsible for NBC's Olympic coverage, to an August 1995 meeting soon after the Disney-ABC and Westinghouse-CBS mergers. NBC had covered three Olympics since Welch had become CEO and Dick Ebersol wanted to get one more, Sydney in 2000. Wright told Welch that Ebersol wanted to bid on Sydney, not as a purely NBC project, however, but rather as a joint venture with the ABC television network, to minimize the risk. Wright was lukewarm about participating in the joint venture, and Welch shared his feelings. Ebersol also wanted to bid on the Salt Lake City Winter Olympics for the year 2002, but bids were not being accepted yet. Wright was concerned about putting all of his Olympic investment in Sydney. Perhaps NBC could bid on Sydney and Salt Lake City together? It had never been done, but why not? The idea had one big advantage: It could commit the same advertisers to both projects at the same time.

Wright spoke to Welch, vacationing in Nantucket. Welch gave the go-ahead on the spot, providing a GE jet to fly Wright and Falco to present their plan to International Olympic Committee officials, first in Montreal, then later in Sweden. The deal was sewn up—a $1.25 billion package.

Later, Dick Ebersol and the IOC worked out an even larger deal, a $2.3-billion package that gave NBC the rights to cover all Olympics through 2008. By the time ABC, CBS, and Fox woke up, the battle for the Olympic rights was at an end: NBC had secured American television rights to five of the next six Olympics at a cost of $3.55 billion. (CBS had previously bought the rights to the 1998 winter games.) When Welch told the tale of that triumph, he made the point that acting swiftly was the key factor in landing the deal.

Jack Welch's willingness to make decisions quickly on large amounts of money was not easy for him. He acknowledged that, after the decision to dismiss someone, decisions to make large GE investments were the second most difficult to make:

> **Making small calls . . . is the easiest job in the world because I've got a big company. "Small" means investments of a hundred million, fifty million, thirty, seventy million. Making two-billion-dollar swings or five-billion-dollar swings or four-billion-dollar swings . . . where you change the game [is a huge challenge]. Where you risk the image of the company. Where you can tip it upside down.**

THE VIRTUES OF CABLE

Overall, the NBC network enjoyed its most profitable year in 1995 ($738 million); it was the third straight year of double-digit earning increases, 7.6 percent of all GE profits. Revenue that year was also a recordbreaking $3.9 billion, 5.6 percent of GE's overall revenues.

Providing the success were the television network, NBC's owned and operated stations, and CNBC, its business and financial news network. NBC also captured every prime-time ratings "sweeps" and was the only broadcast network to show ratings growth in 1995. The year 1996 was the most profitable in the seventy-year history of NBC.

But NBC's greatest victory was the joint-venture deal that Bob Wright negotiated with Bill Gates of Microsoft that enabled NBC to create a news channel with no cash outlay. Thus it was in July 1996 that MSNBC Cable, a twenty-four-hour news-and-information channel, and MSNBC on the Internet, a comprehensive, interactive, on-line news service, debuted. MSNBC got under way with 22 million subscribers, the largest subscriber base ever for a new cable service; it had commitments to reach more than 55 million households by 1999. Fox News Network had stalled by February 1997; it reached only 19 million homes. Wright had made his fledgling network, MSNBC, the clear number two after CNN.

Bob Wright drove NBC to its fourth consecutive year of record revenues and earnings, with more than $5 billion in revenues and an estimated $960 million in operating profits for 1996. NBC's profits from the network alone were at $500 million. Nearly $500 million more came from cable and television station operations.

By 1997, NBC had become one of General Electric's most lucrative businesses. Wright had cut NBC's bloated workforce from 8,000 to fewer than 5,000 full-time jobs, at a savings of $120 million in overhead.

A SHOW ABOUT NOTHING

One of the major reasons for NBC's prosperity in 1997 was the weekly sitcom *Seinfeld*, a program that has made television history. While some, including the cast, joked that *Seinfeld* was essentially a "show about nothing," its fast pace, clever lines, and well-constructed plots made it a fixture in nearly every American family's television-viewing week.

NBC had to pay $120 million to bring *Seinfeld* back for its ninth season in the fall of 1997 (over 10 percent of NBC's entire prime-time budget); the investment paid off: NBC was raking in $180 million from advertising on the program alone. *Seinfeld* became the first television series to command more than $1 million a minute for advertising. Thanks to *Seinfeld* and the demographics it delivered to advertisers, the network in 1996 was seven times as profitable as the only other network in the black, ABC.

Ironically, *Seinfeld* got off to a shaky start when it first aired in 1989, and for the first four years its ratings were only so-so. It became a hit in 1993 only when NBC scheduled it after the highly popular *Cheers* on Thursday nights.

In late December 1997, Jerry Seinfeld let it be known that he wanted to discontinue the show at the end of the 1997–1998 season. So crucial was *Seinfeld* to NBC that Welch himself intervened—in vain, as it turned out. Seinfeld's argument—that he wanted to end the show when the crowds were still applauding—undoubtedly made little sense to Welch. Would he have "retired" an aircraft engine or a light bulb that was dominating its market and gave every indication of continuing to dominate it for the next few years?

SPREADING THE CULTURE

Jack Welch turned NBC around by choosing the right people to run it. Welch loves what Wright did for NBC:

> **Bob Wright is like an orchestra conductor in that he's able to take extreme egos and he's very self-effacing. He doesn't need a lot of stroking. He's very self-confident, very capable. He gives [his team] room. The idea of taking three producers, all well known, all big-leaguers, and giving them big platforms, and letting them go—that was a courageous and brilliant move.**

Welch had done just what critics feared he would do: importing GE's hard-driving culture to NBC. And he did it after confronting—and ultimately winning over—people both inside and outside NBC who argued forcefully that because television was a uniquely creative business, the traditional rules that applied to all other businesses didn't apply, and wouldn't work, at NBC.

One traditional rule was keeping costs down. NBC news executives thought the idea of saving money irrelevant to the news business. Welch disagreed—and won—paring $400 million from the operation over the years.

It was often heard around NBC that Welch and Wright knew nothing about how to run a television network. Welch addressed this point:

> **People say, "Jack, how can you be at NBC? You don't know anything about dramas or comedies." Well, I can't build a jet engine, either. I can't build a turbine. Our job at GE is to deal with resources—human and financial. The idea of getting great talent, giving them all the support in the world, and letting them run is the whole management philosophy of GE, whether it's in turbines, engines, or a network.**

So Bob Wright and his senior executives run NBC "the GE Way": thinking strategically, globally, long run. People who are hired at NBC are expected to be strong and self-confident. They are expected to encourage speed and simplicity, to have no love of bureaucracy. This helps to explain why NBC has done so well.

Welch and Wright, facing a reality that others preferred to ignore, tamed the NBC network. Welch proudly contemplated NBC's accomplishments and acknowledged that GE's sometimes bitter struggle with NBC executives over cost cutting and other issues was a thing of the past:

> **Don't forget, after a decade, you end up with a team that's your team. We don't have people around there who thought being capable was stupid. I remember people who said, "Why are we doing this?" Eventually an organization becomes a group of bright people who buy into the values. The naysayers sort of look silly in an organization after time.**

When Jack Welch bought NBC in the mid-1980s, people wondered why he chose a business that seemed so unlike all the other GE businesses. When NBC seemed to flounder in the early 1990s, there were a lot of "I told you so's," and reports surfaced repeatedly that Welch wanted to sell the network. But many people did not understand a simple truth: Jack Welch had no desire to part with the network. From the day GE took it on, he believed that he had done the right thing. And he liked NBC, liked all the public attention its people and products attracted. He liked the idea that GE could produce turbines and light bulbs, locomotives and power-generating equipment, but it could also produce *ER* and *Seinfeld*, the *Today* show and the Olympics.

He was confident that GE's way was the winning way—that it would be possible to turn NBC around by putting the right people in the right jobs and giving them the space and resources to do their thing. It didn't hurt that a Jerry Seinfeld came along, or that the network's sports lineup was masterfully crafted, or that the news division was picking up viewers. But Jack Welch prefers to think that GE turned NBC around, because the network had begun to follow the GE Way. The rest is television history.

In 2003, Welch's decision to "fix" NBC rather than sell it looked very good. Early that year, NBC reported record revenues of $7.1 billion, a 24 percent increased over 2001; and an operating profit of $1.7 billion, up 18 percent. Among the contributing factors were its improved performance in the advertising market and its broadcast of the 2002 Winter Olympics.

The Jack Welch GE Way Prescription for Fixing a Business:

➤ Make an overall survey of your businesses and decide which you want to keep and which you want to salvage.

➤ In deciding that it is worth keeping a business, even though it requires much effort, draw up a list of what needs to be fixed. Most likely finding new talent at the top will be uppermost in your mind.

➤ Search for the best possible talent to run the business and then let those new business leaders manage without your personal intrusion and interference.

➤ At all times, the secret to your fixing the business will be getting costs in line. So always pay attention to the way money is spent within the business.

CHAPTER 9

DON'T FOCUS ON
THE NUMBERS

*Numbers aren't the vision; numbers are
the product. I never talk about numbers.*

HOW OFTEN HAVE YOU HEARD one of your bosses say,
"We've got to produce better numbers. We've just got to."

That's the extent of the boss's management philosophy—egging on his troops to produce larger revenues, larger profits. You don't dare blame your numbers-fixated boss for having such a clear-cut goal—and for repeating it so often.

The trouble is, after a while, "numbers-speak" gets boring, not to mention unnerving, for the troops being asked to make good on those lofty financial goals.

But worst of all, the fact is that numbers have little to do with creating a vision or fulfilling a mission; they don't instill values into the hearts and minds of the employees, and they don't provide much help in living up to those values or carrying out the vision. In short, it's not management philosophy; it's just a lot of cheerleading.

Here's a **self-assessment exercise** that should help you determine whether you are obsessive about numbers:

1. Do you believe that coming in with the right numbers is all that counts in determining your job performance?

   Yes   No

2. Do you spend hours working out "what-if" scenarios on your computer, hoping to get the numbers to look better?

   Yes   No

3. Do you encourage your colleagues to think about other things than just the numbers, such as how to find more talented managers and develop greater teamwork?

   Yes   No

If you answered the first two questions in the negative and the third affirmatively, you are close to the model leader that Jack Welch has in mind, at least with respect to downplaying a business's numbers. But you are not quite there yet.

To be sure, Welch mentioned the numbers—in every speech, in every Letter to Share Owners, in every talk to financial analysts. And why should he not have? He was proud of how much he accomplished in his two decades as chairman and CEO of General Electric.

Numbers Aren't the Vision

But he did not dwell on the numbers. He refused to get bogged down in them. That's not what leaders do. Leaders lead. And the only way to lead, as far as Welch was concerned, was to teach a clear-cut, consistent, well-thought-out management philosophy. The only way to lead was to focus on company values:

> **Numbers aren't the vision; numbers are the product.**
> **We always say that if you had three measurements to live**
> **by, they'd be employee satisfaction, customer satisfaction,**
> **and cash flow.**

When Welch talked to financial analysts, to the GE board, or to GE's junior executives at the Crotonville Leadership Development Center, he talked values, not numbers. Even his handwritten notes to employees referred to those values. But nowhere was Welch's dislike of numbers plainer than in his annual Letter to Share Owners.

Since the elusive chairman rarely gave interviews or speeches, Welch's letter became one of his primary vehicles for transmitting his business strategies to GE—and to the business world at large. Welch himself considered this letter one of the most important events of his year.

In the early years of his chairmanship, Welch's Letter to Share Owners was fairly straightforward and to the point; he would discuss GE's performance over the past year, and that was usually about it. But by the late 1980s the letter had become a major platform for disseminating Welch's business ideas and management strategies.

LET'S GET ON TO THE IMPORTANT STUFF

Most of the Letters to Share Owners began with a nod to the numbers: "In 1996, your company had its best year ever." Or, "Your company had a terrific 1995." Or, "GE had a great year in 1994." And after each of these brief sentences, Welch backed up his introductory statements with proof through the numbers of why and how GE had done so well.

But he quickly segued into his favorite part of the letter, the part that took up almost 95 percent of the document: a discussion on the company's values.

Here's an example, from the 1990 letter: "Those are the numbers, and we are pleased with them. For the remainder of our letter, we would like to share with you the progress we continue to make in turning our 1980s vision into reality and the promise we see in the vision we outlined last year for our Company in the 1990s." In other words, let's get on to the important stuff.

Just as significantly, when a list of GE's values was compiled, there was never a direct reference to the business numbers. Rather, leaders who adhered to GE's values were expected to create a clear, simple, reality-based, customer-focused vision; they were supposed to have a passion for excellence; to stimulate and relish change; to have enormous energy. What Jack Welch did not say, in compiling that list of values, perhaps because it was all too obvious, was that anyone at GE who adhered to these values was going to *automatically* help in the overall effort to produce the outstanding numbers for which the company strived.

Welch's business philosophy focused on people, not numbers.

He urged GE employees to face reality; to lead, not manage; to change before it was necessary; to be boundaryless; to pursue simplicity; to be self-confident. He never said, Get your numbers up. He knew that it was unrealistic to expect workers to attain Super Bowl-like financial results year after year. Even if they worked around the clock, there were simply too many external factors at work—an unanticipated new product introduced by a rival, a sudden surge of inflation, bad weather—that rendered it impossible to make the numbers.

Let's be clear: Welch *did* care about the bottom line, even if he would deny it. He said he took little comfort from what the company had done in the past on his watch. This was just his way of emphasizing the company's culture. But don't believe for a second that he did not carefully monitor results. He assumed that if he could get his people to come up with the right business values—and integrate them into their behavior—GE's financial record would shine.

PLAYING UP THE "SOFT STUFF"

That's why he talked mostly about what he called the "soft stuff"—the company's values and culture. That's why he would spend lots of ink in his Letter to Share Owners on the notion of a "boundaryless" company, or on the virtues of GE's Work-Out program or quality initiative. For Welch, playing up the soft stuff was key to taking GE to even greater heights in the future. For a GE business leader, coming up with a strong, market-leading product was crucial. So was knowing how to market that product. But to Jack Welch, it was absolutely essential for a leader to buy into the company's value scheme—its corporate culture, if you will—and be able to sell those values to everyone else.

Delivering the numbers was simply not enough. GE business leaders who brought home the numbers but fell short of living up to the company's values found themselves out of a job. That may sound harsh. After all, wasn't making the numbers the most important goal for any manager? Maybe for most managers, but not for Jack Welch:

> **Even senior people with good results, doing great jobs in terms of numbers but not walking the talk, have to be removed to support our values. We have to part company.**

Welch provided one further example of how numbers did not really seem to matter to him. When it was suggested that people listened to his business ideas because of his strong financial performance at the company, he recoiled, saying simply that it was for others to say whether GE had done well. But hadn't Welch himself said back in the 1980s that he wanted to make GE the most competitive enterprise on earth? Wasn't he saying then that he wanted GE to improve its numbers? Yes, he replied, but "I'll never get it there. Because if I ever think I've got it there I'm dead."

Still, there were many people impressed by GE's great numbers who might have looked at its results and said, "Well, I guess that Welch has exceeded his own wildest dreams." Such talk irked the chairman. He did not want to say anything that made it sound as if he were satisfied with where he had taken GE. So he made a point of telling people that he took no comfort in where GE was at any given moment.

Ironically, Welch had been accused of putting pressure on his managers to make their numbers:

- By insisting that his businesses become, and remain, number one or number two in their markets
- By making it clear that he wanted only A-level managers at GE
- By insisting that his business leaders stretched and sought to reach financial results that were above and beyond their yearly budgets

■ By demanding that business leaders adhered to GE values—or faced dismissal

---

The Jack Welch GE Way Prescription for Not Stressing the Numbers:

➤ There will be great temptation to evaluate your own performance by whether or not you bring in the numbers. Don't confine yourself to such thinking. It's too limiting and it's self-defeating.

➤ Focus on other things besides the numbers, such as trying to achieve some or all of the company's core values, and your colleagues will have a higher esteem for you.

➤ Of course, you can't completely dispense with the numbers. That would be foolish. Just don't give them such priority that you fail to deliver on the things that really matter to the company in the long run—implementing its culture, its business philosophy, its values.

CHAPTER 10

PLAGIARIZE—IT'S LEGITIMATE: CREATE A LEARNING CULTURE

The operative assumption today is that someone, somewhere, has a better idea

*I*N THE LATE 1980s AND EARLY 1990s, Jack Welch pushed for an open and informal GE.

In the mid-1990s, he began to focus on the need for GE employees to learn from one another—and from outsiders. He liked to say that GE's core competence was sharing ideas across businesses, across what he called the "boundaryless organization," and that the company viewed itself as a series of laboratories that shared ideas, financial resources, and managers.

It was critical for GE to be open so that it could learn, both from within and from without:

> **We soon discovered how essential it is for a multi-business company to become an open, learning organization. The ultimate competitive advantage lies in an organization's ability to learn and to rapidly transform that learning into action.**

AN APPETITE FOR IDEAS

It was the Work-Out program of the early 1990s that gave birth to GE's voracious appetite for new ideas. This program put to rest the long-held view that only the CEO and GE's senior management knew what was best for its employees. By the late 1990s, the Work-Out process had permeated GE's culture.

Welch had been talking about a learning culture for years, but called it something else in his early days as GE chairman. Back in 1990 he talked about "integrated diversity," describing it as the "elimination of boundaries between businesses and the transferring of ideas from one place in the company to another."

Here's a **self-assessment exercise** to test your own ability to look for new ideas:

1. When a new idea is presented to you, do you applaud the person making the suggestion?

    Yes   **No**

2. Do you believe that you as the business leader can provide all the answers for your company?

    Yes   **No**

3. Do you have an institutionalized program for assuring that new ideas are proposed and find their way to the top of the business?

    Yes   **No**

If you answered no to questions 1 and 3, and yes to question 2, you have a certain way to go before you can truly be described as open to new ideas.

GE'S UNIQUENESS

A large company like GE has access to a whole world of ideas, but the only way to turn that into a competitive advantage is to develop a pervasive, insatiable thirst for those ideas; in effect, there could be no assumption that the GE Way was the only way, or even the best way. Welch observed:

> **The operative assumption today is that someone, somewhere, has a better idea; and the operative compulsion is to find out who has that better idea, learn it, and put it into action—fast. The quality of an idea does not depend on its altitude in the organization . . . An idea can be from any source.**

How, some asked, could an employee in one business make use of an idea from another GE business if those businesses are so radically different? Wasn't GE simply an unfocused conglomerate with no real coherence?

Welch's reply was that the businesses were not all that different from each other—that business was really simple. GE, he liked to say, knows how to move money and people. Ideas, though, are very hard to move.

Welch was not embarrassed to admit, as he did in his Letter to Share Owners in 1993, that GE had benefited from a flood of ideas mined from other companies. It had adapted new product introduction techniques from Chrysler and Canon, effective sourcing techniques from GM and Toyota, and quality initiatives from Motorola and Ford. (Speaking of the quality program, Welch crowed: "I'm very proud of the fact that we didn't invent it. Motorola invented it. Allied followed up with it. And we've taken it. That's a badge of honor. That's not something bad. That's a great thing to do.")

Welch also noted with great pride that GE businesses shared many attributes, including technology, design, personnel compensation and evaluation systems, manufacturing practices, and customer and country knowledge:

- Gas Turbines shared manufacturing technology with Aircraft Engines
- Motors and Transportation Systems worked together on new locomotive propulsion systems
- Lighting and Medical Systems collaborated to improve x-ray tube processes.

■ GE Capital provided innovative financing packages that helped all GE businesses

For example, GE Capital was able to obtain solid market intelligence from GE Power Systems, which, because it builds power plants, is well acquainted with the utility industry. GE Capital was able to generate new business after it learned that Power Systems was having problems with some of its backroom operations. Evidently Power was looking for a way to outsource some of its more troublesome backroom activities, such as billing and collection. When GE Capital's Retailer Financial Services group, which handles billing and collections for 75 million store-brand credit cards, learned of this it sprang into action to secure the account—and a new business opportunity for GE Capital.

Another example of the GE learning culture in action took place in Orlando in March 1997. Welch was meeting with salespeople from Medical Systems. After he and other executives made their presentations, a young salesman stood up and complained that he and his colleagues were not getting paid; their paychecks were showing up late week in and week out. And because he wasn't getting paid on time, he was having a hard time supporting his family. Other companies might have fired the man for complaining directly to the CEO.

But four days later the vice president of sales penned Welch a note saying that the problem had been fixed, and also noted that he had called the man to thank him "and make sure he understood thoroughly how proud I was of him for raising the issue." Welch sent a "modest CEO Award of $1,000" to the young sales representative as a reward for having the courage to speak up. Call this brashness on the part of the salesman, call it crazy, call it what you will. Welch boasts that the outspoken young man helped GE in its quest to create a learning culture.

To encourage a learning culture, Welch believed in compensating his employees generously, but he made it clear that they were being rewarded for teamwork and for sharing ideas. How generously were GE executives being paid? When he became vice chairman in 1979, Welch possessed fewer than 10,000 GE stock options. When he became CEO in 1981, only 200 executives had been awarded stock options. In the late 1990s, when an employee became vice chairman, he probably had close to a million options! By the end of 1997, some 27,000 GE employees had been awarded stock options, and employee investment in GE stock through 401k plans had increased fivefold: from $2 billion in 1991 to $10 billion in late 1997. These numbers certainly bear out the fact that Welch was willing to spend lavishly on what he deems GE's most valuable resource: its people.

THE MOST KNOWLEDGEABLE PEOPLE IN THE WORLD

How could Welch ensure that knowledge was shared between and among the various GE businesses? Perhaps the best way was through the Corporate Executive Council (CEC), a forum of senior GE executives that met for three solid days every quarter, the first annual session taking place on March 15th. That date was not arbitrary; the CEC met a few weeks before the end of each business quarter.

Next to the board, the CEC was the most senior GE forum. It included some twenty-five to thirty people: Jack Welch, the vice chairmen, the twelve business leaders, the five senior corporate officers, and many of the seventeen corporate staff officers. From time to time junior executives were asked to give presentations to the CEC.

In the 1980s, the CEC meetings were held at Fairfield headquarters; later, they were moved to Crotonville. Welch felt that the informal, campus-like atmosphere of the Leadership Development Center encouraged better exchanges among the business leaders.

The CEC began its sessions with dinner on Monday night, followed by informal gatherings. Sessions were held in one of two seminar rooms: the Cave or the Lyceum. The Tuesday session got under way at 8 A.M. and ran until 6 P.M., with one break for lunch. Welch always started off the session, but he seldom opened the same way twice. Sometimes he kicked things off by doing an encore of the slide presentation that he presented to the GE board the week before. Or he might opt to recount the details of a recent visit he'd made to a particular GE business. Or he might launch into a discourse on the U.S. and world economy. All of this just to get the ball rolling!

Then the business leaders deliver in-depth quarterly and annual performance forecasts for their respective divisions. Included in this discussion were war stories on big-ticket sales and accounts, with plenty of details on why a particular sale was won or lost. They also discussed interesting new technological developments or product breakthroughs, as well as new alliances, acquisitions, or dispositions.

While all of this was serious business, the entire session was surprisingly informal. There was a great deal of give and take, with the speaker responding to questions and comments off the cuff. The GE business leaders were also asked to comment on how several companywide initiatives affected their businesses. Some ideas were picked up, others discarded. There was no pressure from Welch to adopt every new "best practice" aired at these sessions. All Welch wanted his top staff to do was generate ideas and implement those they liked.

There were three more CEC sessions later in the year: in mid-June, mid-September, and mid-December. No one sat at the meetings taking notes or recording the sessions. The last thing Welch wanted was for his business leaders to be bogged down in more paper. The idea behind CEC was to provide a learning experience, a meaningful forum in which to exchange ideas, not just another routine gathering that added to the bureaucratic burden.

Welch boasted that when CEC members left after forty-eight hours they might not be the smartest people in the world, but they were the most knowledgeable:

> **We have been exposed to all these relevant topics. What's happening in China? What's happening in this business or that business? For forty-eight hours people share ideas, all knowing that everything counts toward the whole . . . It's like a family clubhouse. We have a great time. I sit in the corner and facilitate ideas.**

When a reporter noted that some people felt a single-product company was stronger than a multibusiness company, Welch refuted that assertion, observing that single-product organizations like IBM, Sears Roebuck, and Kodak had been experiencing trouble:

> **That's because their organizations are closed. People only communicate within their divisions. When they're on the way up, they think they're invincible. Some business is always in trouble at GE. But we've got experience that can be used to help divisions that are down. A decade ago, you used to keep your ideas to yourself at GE. Now, you're rewarded for how many ideas you exchange.**

Learning Culture Pressures

The learning culture produced its own built-in pressures. The CEC created a burden on all those at GE not attending the meetings. They waited and wondered what new ideas would emerge from the forum, what new ideas their CEO would want implemented tomorrow as a result of attending the CEC. The employees wanted to be the ones to initiate a "best practice." They did not want to be told by their CEO about some great new idea that exists at some other GE business.

The Jack Welch GE Way Prescription for Creating a Learning Culture:

➤ The best way to run a company is to convince yourself that you do not have all the answers.

➤ The right answers are out there—somewhere. The trick is to find them and, once they're found, implement them as quickly as possible.

➤ Taking other people's ideas may seem like plagiarism, but it's not. It's legitimate.

PART

FORGING THE BOUNDARYLESS ORGANIZATION

We had to get rid of anything that was getting in the way of being informal, of being fast, of being boundaryless.

CHAPTER 11

GET RID OF THE MANAGERS, GET RID OF THE BUREAUCRACY

Every layer is a bad layer. The world is moving at such a pace that control has become a limitation. It slows you down.

W*HEN JACK WELCH TOOK OVER IN THE EARLY 1980s,* General Electric appeared to be one of the strongest companies in the United States. It was certainly not in the throes of a crisis.

Still, Welch decided to act, and act decisively. Fearing GE's rivals, he wanted to make the company more competitive. To achieve that goal, Welch felt he needed a sleek, aggressive General Electric, and this meant downsizing many of GE's 412,000 employees. At the time, no other American business leader was prepared to take so bold a step.

"TAMPERING" WITH GENERAL ELECTRIC

Until the early 1980s, the American worker had asserted a right to a job for life, and he or she pretty much could depend upon lifelong job security. Welch countered that, with a company's survival at stake, nothing—including jobs—could be considered sacred. Still, downsizing was the hardest part of his job, he admitted later.

Restructuring in the early 1980s left no facet of General Electric untouched. Every one of its 350 business units was a candidate for the CEO's realignment. In time, he reduced his workforce by almost 35 percent, to 270,000.

The "Welch Revolution" was one of the great shifts in American corporate life. He was accused of being heartless, insensitive, and brutal for tampering with the powerful, 103-year-old General Electric mystique. But tamper he did, earning himself the hated nickname "Neutron Jack." That tag clung for years, like a bad odor that simply would not go away, even though Welch argued constantly that GE's workers were given plenty of notice, treated generously, and provided with retraining.

In the late 1990s Welch noted how times had changed:

> **Today, people sort of get a badge of honor for 10,000 [layoffs]. It's terrible to take out people. It's the worst part of the job. But we had to get rid of anything that was getting in the way of being informal, of being fast, of being boundaryless.**

A BLOW TO BUREAUCRACY

Welch believed that a vast, bloated bureaucracy had grown up at GE and it was choking initiative and enthusiasm. Some saw virtue in the decentralized, bureaucratic system. It created order, provided control.

Nonsense, cried the CEO of General Electric. All it did was promote excessive sluggishness. Soon after taking over, he began to tear that bureaucracy apart, attacking layer upon layer of management that he felt obstructed swift, simple communication.

> **The world is moving at such a pace that control has become a limitation. It slows you down.**

Before Welch started his revolution, the basic task of GE managers was to monitor their subordinates' performance. But that sort of command-and-control management style did not permit managers to spot trouble soon enough. Senior managers were merely firing memos at one another. They prevented the CEO from talking directly with junior managers and rank-and-file workers.

TOO MANY TITLES

To the chairman, all of the control and formality inherent in these management layers sapped entrepreneurial spirit. When Welch became CEO in 1981, an astounding 25,000 employees bore the title of manager. There were some 500 senior managers, 130 at vice president level or higher.

Sector heads, ranked as senior vice presidents, spent three days preparing for a meeting with Welch. But when they did meet, it soon became apparent that they were not well informed. Then they had to spend more time digging up the answers to the pointed questions that he asked. Welch abolished this system, removing layers between himself and the divisional CEOs. The number of management levels between the chairman and those in the field dropped from nine to between four and six a decade later; each business was left with only ten vice presidents, rather than the usual fifty found at other companies the size of GE.

Here is a quick **self-assessment exercise** to determine whether your company is as lean as it could be.

1. Have you added any layers of bureaucracy to your company in the past twelve months?

         Yes   No

2. Do your vice presidents and their staffs continually meet with and send memos to one another?

         Yes   No

3. Do you have multiple direct reports?

         Yes   No

If you answered yes to all three questions, you will want to take a fresh look at your company's bureaucracy and devise ways to remove some layers. Welch had a name for his attack upon GE's bureaucracy: *delayering*. Without all those layers, the company could become lean and agile.

Critics argued that delayering reduced necessary command and control. Not so, insisted Welch.

The Jack Welch GE Way Prescription for Delayering:

➤ Delayering is one of the hardest parts of being a leader. But it is vital to eliminate managers who slow down a company and make it less entrepreneurial.

➤ Delayering makes it easier for the CEO to find out what's going on in the company, as there are fewer filters and fewer memos and meetings.

➤ If you want to become a high-performance business leader, you must take a hard look at every layer of management—and then decide where to cut and how to improve communications with the people on the factory floor.

12

C H A P T E R

BE LEAN AND AGILE LIKE A SMALL COMPANY

*Small companies move faster. They
know the penalties for hesitation in
the marketplace.*

JACK WELCH BELIEVED THAT TO SURVIVE in an
increasingly competitive world, large companies like General
Electric had to stop behaving and thinking like . . . large companies.
They had to get lean and agile. They had to start thinking like a
small company.

To create a leaner GE, Welch delayered; then he removed the
entire second and third echelons of management—the sectors and
groups. In the 1980s, business leaders had reported to senior vice
presidents, who reported to executive vice presidents—all of
whom had staffs of their own. Welch changed that: The business
leaders would report directly to the three people who occupied the
CEO's office—Welch and his two vice chairmen:

> **We found ourselves in the early 1980s with corporate
> and business staffs that were viewed—and viewed them-
> selves—as monitors, checkers, kibitzers, and approvers.**

The staff now sees itself as facilitator, adviser, and partner of operations.

Here is a brief **self-assessment exercise** to determine whether you are helping your large company behave like a small one.

1. Are there management layers that you could cut that would enable you as the business leader to have direct contact with more junior managers?

         Yes   No

2. Are you constantly looking for deadwood among the rank-and-file so that you can create a leaner company?

         Yes   No

3. Are you able to ward off pressure to expand your senior management?

         Yes   No

If you answered all three questions in the positive, you appear to understand what is required to build a lean, agile company.

THE VIRTUES OF BEING SMALL

Jack Welch was not against bigness per se. He loved the idea that GE was one of the world's largest corporations and getting larger every day. But he wanted GE to avoid the inherent pitfalls of being big. Big companies have a tendency to become bureaucratic wastelands. They move too slowly, think too slowly, and, more important, *act* too slowly. Trying to build a sleek, competitive enterprise while saddled by those red-tape accoutrements is like trying to win a race wearing cement shoes.

Welch felt that small, sleek companies have huge competitive advantages: They communicate better; they move faster; they make it easier to identify the most talented leaders.

And, finally, small companies waste less. They spend less time in endless reviews and approvals and politics and paper drills. Their people are free to direct their en-

ergy and attention toward the marketplace rather than fighting bureaucracy.

SPEED IS THE KEY INGREDIENT

Welch understood that small companies fear bureaucracy and all that usually accompanies it. Employees of small companies must be fast on their feet all the time, or risk falling into the same traps as larger companies. Speed "is the indispensable ingredient in competitiveness," said Welch. "Speed keeps businesses—and people—young. It's addictive."

Welch noted that companies appeared to follow predictable life cycles. At the beginning, new businesses are gripped with an urgency to get to the marketplace. In such an environment, bureaucracy has a hard time getting a foothold—just as ice cannot form in a fast-moving stream. But, as institutions grow and become more comfortable, their priorities shift:

- From speed to control
- From leading to managing
- From winning to conserving what they have won
- From serving the customer to serving the bureaucracy

Welch said that if you were not fast you could not win:

> **You must get products to market faster and response from customers quicker. You've got to make decisions fast. If you're not boundaryless, and you've got a bunch of layers, that's like going out in the cold with six sweaters on. Your body doesn't know what the temperature is.**

With speed a cardinal virtue at GE, Welch and his team made closing a deal in record time a badge of honor. They took great pride in talking about how in 1989 they took only three days to seal an alliance with the British firm GEC—a deal that increased their share of the European market for four of its businesses: Medical Systems, Appliances, Industrial and Power Systems, and Electrical Distribution and Control. And they loved to point to 1995, when it took NBC only a weekend to sew up the exclusive rights to televise five of the next six Olympic Games for $4 billion. GE is proud of the fact that NBC was able to move so quickly, despite the size of the deal. After all, how many other companies could decide to spend $4 *billion* in a single weekend?

In his 1992 Letter to Share Owners, Welch noted what it was about small companies that he admired. It was that most small companies were uncluttered, simple, and informal. They thrive on passion and ridicule bureaucracy. They find and implement good ideas. Small companies dream big dreams and set the bar high. They are not interested in increments or fractions.

> **We love the way small companies communicate: with simple, straightforward, passionate argument rather than jargon-filled memos, "putting it in channels," "running it up the flagpole," and worst of all, the polite deference to the small ideas that too often come from big offices in big companies.**
>
> **Everyone in a small company knows the customers—their likes, dislikes, and needs—because the customers' thumbs up or down means the difference between a small company becoming a bigger company tomorrow—or no company at all. It comes down to something very simple: Small companies have to face into the reality of the market every day, and when they move, they have to move with speed. Their survival in on the line.**

The Jack Welch GE Way Prescription for Thinking Like a Small Company:

➤ The goal of a business leader is certainly to make the business grow and be profitable.

➤ But as you grow, don't lose sight of the virtues of what small businesses offer and what they do better than their larger counterparts.

➤ Don't permit the attributes of bigness to stand in your way, to overwhelm you, to weigh you down like a cement-shoed runner.

CHAPTER 13

TEAR DOWN THE BOUNDARIES

Our people must be as comfortable in Delhi and Seoul as they are in Louisville or Schenectady.

*J*ACK WELCH FELT THAT THERE WERE FAR TOO MANY *BOUNDARIES* within General Electric. Everywhere he turned, he found boundaries:

- Between management layers
- Between engineers and marketing people
- Between GE and its customers
- Between full-time and part-time GE employees
- Between GE and the whole outside community

Here is a brief **self-assessment exercise** to help you become boundaryless:

1. Do your engineers and marketing personnel communicate easily and comfortably with one another?

   Yes   No

2. Do your customers feel that they have an open door in terms of communicating comments or complaints?

   Yes   No

3. Do you feel that the outside community has a sound understanding of your company's objectives?

Yes   No

If you answered all three in the negative, you have a lot of work
to do to become boundaryless.

Boundaries, barriers—same thing. Welch hated boundaries
and wanted to get rid of them. They slowed down the company.
They complicated matters. They got in the way. Welch felt that the
boundaries between GE and the outside world were due to a longstanding GE belief that he labeled the "not invented here" (NIH)
syndrome: if an idea is not invented at General Electric, it's worth-
less. Welch hated NIH thinking.

Boundarylessness, an awkward term that Welch coined, defined the GE to which Welch aspired: an open, informal company
where employees can move swiftly and effortlessly and connect to
the outside world just as quickly and effectively. The fewer the
boundaries, the higher the productivity, Welch argued.

> **We've got to create what we call a boundaryless com-
> pany. We no longer have the time to climb over barriers
> between functions like engineering and marketing, or be-
> tween people—hourly, salaried, management, and the like.
> Geographic barriers must evaporate. Our people must be
> as comfortable in Delhi and Seoul as they are in Louisville
> or Schenectady.**

Boundarylessness had been a key strategy in Welch's effort to
achieve General Electric's productivity goals. But the strategy
called for much more than simply eliminating bureaucratic waste
and boosting productivity.

Welch's view of the 1990s was based on the premise that the
workplace needs to be liberated. Workers should no longer be
told what to do, but should be empowered and given responsibility. In this brave new world all employees are permitted to partic-
ipate in decision making and have full access to vital information
needed to make those decisions. Welch would move toward
boundarylessness by liberating the workers and letting them
speak for themselves.

WORKING WITH EVERYONE

Every once in a while, the General Electric chairman himself would confront examples of boundaries—and act immediately to tear them down. He once discovered that whenever he called a meeting, certain GE staffers spent countless hours preparing page after page of possible answers to questions he might throw at them. This canned material represented a "boundary" that the staffers were imposing between themselves and Welch. He told the staff that he didn't want them going through those preparations. It wasted too much time.

But even after Welch put an end to that practice, the staff was still concerned that he might ask them something they couldn't answer. So they stationed an employee outside the meeting, ready to research an answer as quickly as possible. That employee became another boundary, preventing the staff from dealing with Welch directly. Once he caught on to that boundary, Welch halted that practice as well.

The next time there was a meeting, the CEO put a question to one staff member, a question he couldn't answer. "I don't know the answer," the person confessed, bewildered, but unable to think of what else to say. Welch applauded. Then he said, "That's OK, but make sure you find out and let me know." The chairman was thrilled. He had created a sense of boundarylessness among the staff that would pay off in less time wasted, less unnecessary effort expended.

IT'S HOW WE ACT

With the creation of the Corporate Executive Council in 1986, GE's senior executives began engaging in boundaryless behavior—talking to one another directly and informally, learning from one another, adapting "best practices" for their own use.

But Welch's most aggressive attempt to rid GE of its boundaries was the launching of the massive companywide initiative called

Work-Out in 1990. Welch noted in 1996 that Work-Out had elim-inated insularity at GE by going after NIH and eradicating it. Through Work-Out, GE began to systematically explore the world's best companies for better ways of doing things. That cre-ated the basis for GE's learning culture—another critical Welch business strategy of the late 1990s.

While the town meeting approach was originally designed to dismantle GE's internal ceilings and walls, Welch began to sense that the Work-Out process would also help to get rid of external walls by strengthening ties with customers and suppliers.

Welch said that the development of a boundaryless learning culture is the most important product of Work-Out and that cul-ture defines how GE employees should behave. The removal of walls, Welch wrote in his 1993 Letter to Share Owners, meant that

> **. . . we involve suppliers as participants in our design and manufacturing processes rather than treat them as ven-dors, left to cool their heels in waiting rooms. It means having major launch customers like British Airways, Tokyo Electric Power, or CSX in the room and involved in the de-sign of a new jet engine, a revolutionary gas turbine, or a new AC locomotive, or a panel of doctors helping us de-velop a new ultrasound system.**

The Jack Welch GE Way Prescription for Becoming Boundaryless:

➤ If you're a business leader, at whatever level, you've got to ask yourself: What parts of my business are slowing us down? What parts are bottling us up?

➤ You must systematically dismantle all the obstacles in-side your business that hamper the successful manufac-ture and marketing of products.

➤ Get rid of the roadblocks—you will find that your busi-ness will speed up and your employees become more productive.

P A R T IV

HARNESSING YOUR PEOPLE FOR COMPETITIVE ADVANTAGE

*My whole job is people. I can't design an
engine. I have to bet on people.*

14
C H A P T E R

THREE SECRETS: SPEED, SIMPLICITY, AND SELF-CONFIDENCE

Bureaucracy is terrified by speed and hates simplicity.

*T*HE RESTRUCTURING EFFORT OF THE 1980s proved to be a crucial element in creating the streamlined GE that Welch knew was needed.

But he sensed that to transform GE into a world-class company, he would have to devise a new strategy that was capable of supercharging an arguably weakened workforce. The downsizing had left the two-thirds still employed reeling, consumed by worry over job security. Welch knew that he would have to help diminish the uneasiness and rebuild confidence and self-worth.

In the early 1980s, he had said that the world would soon become far more complex, and history was proving him right. The field of competition had turned into a crowded battleground, as Europe, Korea, and Taiwan joined Japan in the global fray. Simply pursuing more of the hardware solutions of the 1980s—downsizing, plant closings, and so forth—would not be nearly enough to triumph in the cutthroat 1990s:

The competitive world of the Nineties will make the Eighties look like a walk in the park . . . To win we have to find the key to dramatic, sustained productivity growth . . . We have to move from the incremental to the radical, toward a fundamental revolution in our approach to productivity and to work itself—a revolution that must touch every single person in the organization every business day.

SPEED, SIMPLICITY, SELF-CONFIDENCE

He summed up his prescription for winning in three words:

- Speed
- Simplicity
- Self-confidence

If he could get GE employees to work with speed, simplicity, and self-confidence, Welch was confident that the dividends would begin appear on the bottom line. GE would become more productive—and more profitable.

Speed Decreases Control

Welch knew that in order to get speed, *real* speed, decisions at virtually every level would have to be made in minutes, not days or weeks. He also knew that decisions had to be made face-to-face, not memo-to-memo.

In his 1993 Letter to Share Owners, the chairman harped on speed. In fact, in that memorable letter, he talked more about speed and boundarylessness than any other topic. He gave some examples of GE's speed:

- There was a new product announcement at GE Appliances every ninety days—unthinkable years ago
- The GE90, the world's most powerful commercial jet engine, was designed and built in half the normal time

■ Another team developed a breakthrough ultrasound innovation in less than a year and a half; others designed and built a new AC locomotive in eighteen months

In his 1994 Letter to Share Owners, Welch talked about new product introduction as one of the best ways to measure GE's speed. He gave these examples:

■ GE Power Systems, which once took years to develop new products, had designed and brought to market three new gas turbine generators in 1994

■ Product development in Medical Systems had gone from a two-year cycle to less than one, and 70 percent of GE's computed tomography products were less than one year old

SIMPLE ENOUGH FOR COCKTAIL PARTY CHATTER

As for simplicity, Jack Welch proclaimed that business is simple. No matter how different GE businesses seem one from the other, he urged everyone in the company to think simply, to see themselves as performing essentially the same two processes—inputs and outputs—and not to make anything more complicated out of business than that. The inputs were the same, he declared. They were people, energy, and physical space. Some people perform mechanical feats, some do financial tasks, but when you think about what you do conceptually, you're really not doing different things, said Welch. Simplicity is practically an art form, with many definitions:

> **To an engineer, it's clean, functional designs with fewer parts. For manufacturing it means judging a process not by how sophisticated it is, but how understandable it is to those who must make it work. In marketing it means clear messages and clean proposals to consumers and industrial customers. And, most importantly, on an individual, interpersonal level it takes the form of plain speaking, directness—honesty.**

Simplicity is also indispensable to a business leader's most important function: creating and projecting a clear vision, observed Welch:

The leader's unending responsibility must be to remove every detour, every barrier, to ensure that vision is first clear, and then real. The leader must create an atmosphere in the organization where people feel not only free to, but obliged to demand clarity and purpose from their leaders.

A business leader needed what Welch called an overarching message—something big but simple and understandable. Whatever it is—we're going to be number one or number two, or fix/close/sell, or boundaryless—every idea you present must be something you could get across easily at a cocktail party with strangers. If only aficionados of your industry can understand what you're saying, you've blown it.

One of the most difficult things for a manager to do, contended the head of GE, is to reach that all-important threshold of self-confidence in which being simple is comfortable.

Simple messages travel faster, simpler designs reach the market faster, and the elimination of clutter allows faster decision making.

"All this happened in the upper echelons of GE," wrote Welch in his 1995 Letter to Share Owners. "We saw the leadership come alive with energy, excitement, and the crackle of small-company urgency."

SELF-CONFIDENCE: THE ANTIDOTE TO INSECURITY

Welch knew that the survivors were shaken by the massive changes, and above all else were in dire need of a healthy dose of self-confidence: "If we are to create this boundaryless company, we have to create an atmosphere where self-confidence can grow in each . . . of us." The root cause of many of bureaucracy's ills—the bitterness, the turf battles, the in-fighting and pettiness so rife in many organizations—was insecurity, suggested Welch. Insecurity makes people resist change because they see change only as a threat, never as an opportunity. And the way to build self-confidence is to give people a voice, to get them talking and listening to and trusting one another:

> **Self-confidence does not grow in someone who is just another appendage on the bureaucracy, whose authority rests on little more than a title . . . We began to cultivate self-confidence among our leaders by turning them loose, giving them independence and resources, and encouraging them to take big swings.**

A company cannot simply manufacture or distribute self-confidence. But it can provide an atmosphere that affords employees that opportunity to dream, risk, and win—and ultimately earn self-confidence.

The Jack Welch GE Way Prescription for Attaining Speed, Simplicity, and Self-Confidence:

➤ Develop the self-confidence to make meaningful changes in your business.

➤ Develop the self-confidence to simplify and speed up your business procedures.

➤ Speed, simplicity, and self-confidence may sound like dozens of other business aphorisms. But when they are truly encouraged and developed, they are powerful management tools that can help streamline your organization and boost the productivity of your entire workforce.

CHAPTER 15

USE THE BRAINS OF EVERY WORKER—INVOLVE EVERYONE

Get the management layers off their backs, the bureaucratic shackles off their feet, and the functional barriers out of their way.

JACK WELCH'S FIRST REVOLUTION AT GENERAL ELECTRIC brought massive change.

Some 350 businesses were transformed into 13. The core electrical manufacturing businesses were no longer the focus of the company; high-tech and service segments were. Plants were shut, buildings were leveled, existing factories were made state-of-the-art. New plants were built and layers of management were cast aside. The number of employees dropped by a third, from 412,000 to 270,000. Revenues and earnings were on the rise.

Welch called these years the "hardware phase." The hardware phase had made General Electric more competitive, but it also had a totally disorienting effect on employees that had survived the cut but still lived in fear for their jobs. They needed to feel wanted.

A PLAN TO CAPTURE GOOD IDEAS

Welch understood their feelings.

Here's a brief **self-assessment exercise** to determine whether you understand the feelings of your employees:

1. Do you believe that the only good ideas come from senior management?

   Yes   No

2. Do you encourage your rank-and-file to come up with ideas for improving the business to present to senior personnel?

   Yes   No

3. Do you feel proud of an employee, rather than resentful, when that employee steps forward with a way of making your business better?

   Yes   No

If you answered no to the first question and yes to the next two, you display sensitivity toward your employees—and that is a good thing.

Welch understood that he needed to make his employees feel less like overworked cogs in a machine and more like "owners" of the business—like direct participants in running the business. His solution was Work-Out, a program designed to foster, capture, and implement good ideas, regardless of their origin. By getting more involved, Welch argued, employees would be helping to strengthen GE's businesses—and healthy, growing businesses were the best guarantee for job security.

In the past, GE managers had been responsible for improving productivity. "We generally used to tell people what to do," noted Welch. "And they did exactly what they were told to do, and not one other thing." Now this task is shared with the men and women on the factory floor, and "we are constantly amazed by how much people will do when they are *not* told what to do by management." Though he was empowering his employees through Work-Out, Welch didn't want to label the new process *empowerment.* He preferred the phrase *high involvement.*

That doesn't mean abdication of decision-making authority by leadership:

> **We want ideas from everyone. But somebody's got to run the ship. Now, that doesn't mean somebody runs the ship by directing it. Somebody runs the ship with a total input from everyone.**

TOO BAD WE WAITED SO LONG

Welch regretted waiting seven years to empower his workforce, but he felt that starting any earlier did not make sense. There had been too much ferment at GE: Thousands of employees were leaving, while thousands of others were joining the company's ranks.

Welch got the idea for Work-Out one day in September 1988 when he visited Crotonville, GE's Leadership Development Center. On that particular day, Welch was speaking to both upper and lower levels of GE management. Some complained that the real problem lay with their bosses, who they felt did not share GE values and therefore had little interest in improving the day-to-day operations of the company.

Several staffers spelled out the problem for Welch: after all the downsizing and delayering, there were fewer employees left to perform the work. Rather than empathize with their situation, the bosses simply dumped the extra workload on the remaining workers with little or no concern for how that might affect them.

After his appearance at Crotonville, Welch was annoyed. Why, he asked himself, was there no dialogue within those units? Sadly, he knew the answer all too well: Despite all the changes Welch had put into effect, GE was still a giant hierarchy. Senior management only spoke to intermediate management, who only talked to junior management, who were the only ones who seemed to talk to the workers on the factory floor. The floor workers were not expected or encouraged to engage in dialogue with superiors. They were expected to work.

Shouldn't this rigid and archaic chain of command be put to an end? Wasn't it time to harness the talent and energy of all employees and force the bosses to answer the questions raised at Crotonville that day?

It seemed crucial to Welch to get lower-level management on board the GE revolution. The top managers were already there. But lower-level managers remained resistant to change. Welch sensed that the solution lay in getting GE personnel to raise work-related issues with managers back home—instead of with the General Electric chairman: "We have to create an atmosphere where people can speak up to somebody who can do something about their problems." Welch alone couldn't solve those issues.

ENGAGING THE WORKERS' MINDS

Welch wanted GE's business leaders to stand eyeball-to-eyeball with the employees and do something they evidently had not done for quite some time: actually *listen* to them. It was quite likely that managers would resist such dialogue at first. They wouldn't find it easy to turn over the "managing" of the company to unqualified "soldiers."

But he was ready to take the risk, and he put his plan into action. He had a strong conviction that much of the creativity and innovation that drove productivity lay with the men and women closest to the actual work. Welch became very concerned that his managers might stifle the process of high involvement. So, he argued, "If you are controlling two people and just getting them to do what you say, I'd get rid of you and keep those two. If there are three people, I want three ideas. If you're only giving orders, I will get only your ideas. I'd rather select from the ideas of three people. That's GE's basic thinking."

In seeking to engage his workers, Welch appeared to be imposing one more difficult demand on his business leaders. As hard as it was for his managers to fire an employee, it would be almost as difficult to turn over decision making to the workers who remained behind. But that's what Welch wanted. He wasn't advocating empowerment out of some altruistic impulse or some sense that the business leaders weren't as smart as the employees on the factory floor.

No, Jack Welch was saying something else: You simply must treat your employees as an integral part of your business. Do that, and you will find employees responding by becoming more engaged and conscientious. And an engaged, conscientious worker is a more motivated, productive worker.

The Jack Welch GE Way Prescription for High Involvement:

➤ Get workers involved and empowered. That will make them feel important. Every employee wants to feel important to the company.

➤ Workers want to feel needed and important—a simple fact that business leaders can exploit, but that also requires some sacrifice.

➤ Managing less is managing more. And although managing less is not always easy to practice, it has tremendous advantages.

VAL NEEDED?

ower over the topics discussed; how-
he or she sought to level the playing
s were constrained from dominating
others in the room. And, like an um-
f, letting the attendees do most of the
e facilitator would ask the minigroups
nary session, the groups would report
n what the others were discussing.
discussants were expected to evaluate

e, and which did not? Which could
to be kept? The idea was to get peo-

earance, the "boss"—the leader or se-
vay. Not only did bosses have to leave;
ring with the session could jeopardize
osed to take notes during the first two
Welch feared that note taking would
e exercise. During the last few hours
nally permitted back into the meeting
en to their ideas, and respond posi-
osals as possible—on the spot!

ANSWERING

etween the boss and the employees
power, its real significance. For two

16
CHAPTER

TAKE THE "BOSS ELEMENT" OUT OF YOUR COMPANY

You've got to balance freedom with some control, but you've got to have more freedom than you've ever dreamed of.

W ORK-OUT was Jack Welch's bold, ambitious, ten-year program to push cultural change throughout General Electric. Starting in 1989, its primary goal was to broaden the scope of debate throughout the entire company. It also set a high goal of removing the "boss element" from General Electric. Managers were now supposed to listen to employees; they were now given the right—and the responsibility—to come up with their own ideas for solving nagging problems.

While other companies experimented with similar empowerment efforts, GE was the first enterprise to undertake such a program on a companywide scale. Ultimately, of course, the goal of the Work-Out program was to make workers more productive and processes simpler and more clear-cut. Work-Out was designed to reduce, and ultimately eliminate, all of the wasted hours and energy that organizations like GE typically expend in performing day-to-day operations. In Welch's words, Work-Out was meant to help people stop

wrestling with the boundaries, the absurdities that grow in large organizations. We're all familiar with those absurdities: too many approvals, duplication, pomposity, waste.

CONFRONTING THE BOSS FACE-TO-FACE

Work-Out had two defining aspects:

1. Employees had to be able to make suggestions to their bosses face-to-face.
2. Employees had to be able to get a response—on the spot, if possible.

The most appropriate model for Work-Out, one that would help break down the walls of hostility between managers and employees, was the New England town meeting, which had once provided a forum for dialogue between local citizens and town fathers.

The GE "town meetings" (Work-Out sessions) began in March 1989. Welch wanted everyone at GE to have at least a taste of Work-Out by the end of its first year. The program was *not* optional, but the chairman did not live in a fantasy world: he understood that many employees were suspicious of Work-Out, fearing that the program was just another brand of GE downsizing. So in order to soften the blow, he began the program as a volunteer effort.

Before a Work-Out session was to begin, business leaders urged potential participants to brainstorm with colleagues in order to generate additional ideas for the session. Work-Out organizers always urged those attending to feel free to raise any topic they wished.

CHINOS AND T-SHIRTS

The workshops, which usually lasted three days (although some were only two and a half days), were always held off-site, usually at a

WHY IS THAT APPR

The facilitator had no veto ever, like a baseball umpire, field: high-ranking employe the conversation or bullying pire, the facilitator stayed alo talking. From time to time, th to join forces. During this pl back and everyone could lear

Throughout the session, four aspects of the business:

- Reports
- Meetings
- Measurements
- Approvals

Which of these made ser be eliminated and which ha ple talking.

After making an initial ap nior representative—stayed a they were even told that interf their careers. No one was supp days of the Work-Out session add wasteful bureaucracy to t of the third day, the boss was f to confront the employees, li tively to as many of their pro

ONLY THREE WAYS O

It is this final-day encounter that gives Work-Out its speci full days, employees have spent hour upon hour discussing the boss, dissecting his or her strengths and weaknesses. Initiating the process had been none other than Jack Welch himself.

None of this is lost on the participants in Work-Out, and the boss's return to the session is usually a dramatic one. The boss takes a position at the front of the room. Up to this point, that mere act of moving to the front of the room had given the boss an aura of authority, of respect and power. Now the boss stands in front of the employees to listen to *them*. In this final stage of Work-Out, participants put forward their proposals, and the boss is permitted to make only one of three responses:

1. Agree on the spot to implement a proposal.
2. Say no to the proposal.
3. Ask for more information, in effect postponing a decision. If that occurs, the boss must authorize a team to get that information by a certain set date.

Routinely, 80 percent of the proposals receive immediate answers. If additional study is required, the manager has to come up with an answer within one month.

One of the Work-Out participants is selected to prepare a memo on all the proposals discussed (which may be as many as twenty-five), along with the steps to be taken by management as part of determining the feasibility of a particular proposal. The memo is then quickly distributed to all Work-Out participants, who certify that it accurately reflects events at that final session with the boss. Lastly, the memo is circulated to everyone else in that particular GE business. Next to each recommendation is the name of the Work-Out participant who raised the issue—the issue's "champion"—who must then follow up on his or her recommendation and inform the attendees, through the Work-Out leader, of progress.

The goal of Work-Out is to come up with specific, actionable items that leave little room for ambiguity: barred are recommendations that contain vague language, such as "We want to have this new policy." Each recommendation may contain as many as three action items, and each action item must be accompanied by a deadline. Finally, the Work-Out leader assigns a "roadblock buster" who has the task of following up to make sure that each deadline is met.

The Jack Welch GE Way Prescription for Implementing Work-Out:

➤ Choose the issues to be discussed.

➤ Select the appropriate cross-functional team to tackle the problem.

➤ Choose a "champion" who will see any Work-Out recommendations through to implementation.

➤ Let the team meet for three (or two and a half) days, drawing up recommendations to improve your company's processes.

➤ Meet with managers, who make decisions on the spot about each recommendation.

➤ Hold more meetings as required to pursue the implementation of the recommendations.

➤ Keep the process going, with these and other issues and recommendations.

CHAPTER 17

CREATE AN ATMOSPHERE WHERE WORKERS FEEL FREE TO SPEAK OUT

Those who actually did the work . . . had some striking ideas on how things could be done better.

*A*S THE WORK-OUT PROGRAM FIRST GOT UNDER WAY, the invisible walls between managers and employees remained firmly in place, inhibiting a free-flowing dialogue. There were many awkward silences. But here and there, the Work-Out concept began to catch on as someone had the courage to ask a question—and a manager changed a policy on the spot.

Although Work-Out caught on at some of the GE businesses, in the beginning there was no shortage of problems. Union members, who naturally harbored suspicions whenever company executives came forward with an idea, any idea, had become convinced that Welch simply intended to cut payrolls, rather than learn from workers how to improve the company. But eventually these union members—as well as the other participants—realized that he actually meant to turn decision-making power over to the workers.

Of course, not every Work-Out session ran like clockwork. In some sessions, the program was little more than a glorified opportunity for workers to squeal on one another for such infractions as reading a newspaper or "hiding behind" a machine all day instead of working.

Here is a brief **self-assessment exercise** to determine how you as an employee of a large company might be able to introduce change in the company's operations:

1. Does your company have a program that allows you to suggest improvements in its operations?

       Yes   No

2. Do you feel comfortable talking to your boss about ways to improve productivity?

       Yes   No

3. Does your boss regard your suggestions with an open mind?

       Yes   No

If you answered all three questions in the negative, there is certainly room within your organization for a Work-Out program.

RATTLERS AND PYTHONS

At some Work-Out sessions the facilitator broke work issues into two categories: rattlers and pythons. Rattlers were the simple problems, those that could be "shot," like a dangerous rattlesnake, and solved on the spot.

Pythons were issues too complicated to unravel right away, just as no one could easily unravel a coiled python.

One "rattler" involved a young woman who had been publishing a popular plant newspaper, but in doing so had encountered a wall of bureaucracy. GE policy required her to obtain an astounding seven signatures every month in order to get her newspaper published. She pled her case emotionally: "You all like the plant newspaper. It's never been criticized. It's won awards. Why does it take seven signatures?"

Her boss stared at her in amazement. "This is crazy. I didn't know that was the case."

"Well, that's the way it is," she replied.

"OK," the general manager said, "from now on, no more signatures."

The newspaper editor beamed.

At a Work-Out session for the company's communications personnel, a secretary asked why she had to interrupt her own work to empty the "out tray" on her boss's desk. Why couldn't he drop the material off on her desk the next time he left his office? No one had a good answer, and a few steps of unproductive effort were scratched from the secretary's routine—again, on the spot.

At a Work-Out session involving GE Power Generation personnel, someone noted that the Purchasing Department chose welding equipment without conferring with the welders who actually used the equipment. That led to inappropriate equipment being selected for certain tasks. Why not have the welders join the purchasing team when visiting vendors to order equipment?

Without hesitation, the manager said fine.

But pythons proved far more stubborn than rattlers. At one session, a python appeared at a Power Generation Work-Out. Attending the session were personnel in turbine manufacturing, sales, and field service. One gripe came from field service engineers, who complained about having to write mammoth, 500-page reports, which were supposedly needed because they forecast the turbines that might need replacing the next time an outage occurred. Despite the massive effort necessary to prepare such unwieldy documents, no one paid much attention to them. Knowing that, the field service engineers often turned them in as much as six months late, if at all. Eventually, thanks to some intense Work-Out sessions, the gargantuan reports were scrapped and in their place briefer, more up-to-date reports were turned in immediately—and were actually read!

Even as employees were dealing with the trivial, easy issues, Work-Out was giving them an increased sense of participation in their jobs and a good feeling about themselves.

THESE ARE NOT "RAT SESSIONS"

It became a major test of the program to make sure that town meetings did not degenerate into "rat sessions," meetings to find out who was lazy or who hated the boss.

In time, GE's union members began to sense that management's motives were indeed sincere: Their true purpose in Work-Out was to get rid of bad work habits, not simply to uncover laggards. Welch urged GE managers to resist adding up the number of Work-Out sessions they had arranged, convinced that all that extra time and energy could be put to better use elsewhere. "Don't ever tell me you had forty-one Work-Outs," he told them. "I don't want to know."

If the program were working, he noted, it would show up in the only measurement that counted: increased productivity. Still, businesspeople rate success and failure in quantitative terms. Some managers could not help but brag about how many Work-Outs they had under their belts.

By the spring of 1998, nearly every GE employee had taken part in Work-Out sessions.

Work-Out sessions found ways to improve the company, no matter how insignificant the issue. In Louisville, Kentucky, where GE makes appliances, employees at a Work-Out session sought to find ways to improve the environment in Building One, where clothes washers and dryers are made. The place turned into a virtual steam bath in the summer, even before the machines on the assembly lines were turned on! The recommendations were to open some vents that had been closed for years (no one could remember why they had been closed in the first place) and buy a few fans and blowers. As a way of emphasizing their point, Work-Out participants asked their boss to walk out with them to the parking lot, where they took their time setting up easels and flip charts while the boss melted in the noonday sun. The overheated boss got the point and gave a quick OK to cooling off Building One.

Quite a number of the recommendations at Work-Out sessions proved incredibly simple to implement. One computer lab technician, for example, noted that every report printout from his department contained about ten unnecessary pages on it because it first ran out an initial computer code. The Work-Out participants asked him how he might cut this, and he said, "Just hit the suppress button." When one of his managers approached the man and asked him in a friendly manner why he had not told the managers about this before, the man replied, "No one ever asked me."

Here is what Work-Out has accomplished, in Jack Welch's view:

> **As we took down much of the clutter and scaffolding of layers and organizational structure and got rid of the useless noise bureaucracy always generates . . . we started to see deeper into the organization and hear the voices of those who actually did the work, ran the processes . . . and dealt with the customers. They had some striking ideas on how things could be done better.**

Is it possible to measure the success of the Work-Out program? Welch took GE from $25 billion in revenues to nearly $126 billion in the two decades he presided over the company; he made GE the most valuable company in the world. While it's not possible to quantify the financial impact of Work-Out, most would argue that it played a leading role in igniting a revolution at GE, helping thousands of employees feel like they have a stake in the business, like the company really does want to hear what they have to say.

The Jack Welch GE Way Prescription for Building an Effective Program for Listening to Employees:

➤ Employees may be suspicious at first, but put them in a room with the boss and create a situation where they can talk to one another about how to improve operations.

➤ It takes courage from the boss. No business leader is going to find it comfortable—at least at first—to stand in front of employees, be critiqued, and listen to a litany of recommendations for change.

➤ It takes courage from the employees as well. Few employees are going to feel totally relaxed, at least at first, about taking on the boss.

➤ But it can be done. GE has done it—with much to show for opening up its decision-making process to the entire company.

CHAPTER 18

S–T–R–E–T–C–H! REACH FOR THE STARS!

In a boundaryless organization with a bias for speed, decimal points are a bore.

JACK WELCH BELIEVED in a business strategy he called *stretching*. It meant exceeding goals. Often, business leaders exceed goals even as they fall short of the stretch. Welch was fine with that and favored rewarding such efforts. He was against meting out punishment. Only by setting the performance bar high did it become possible to discover people's capabilities.

Welch's notion of "stretch" simply meant figuring out performance targets—on everything from profitability to new product introductions—that were achievable, reasonable, and within GE's scope. It then meant raising sights higher—much higher—toward goals that seemed almost beyond reach, goals that required superhuman effort to achieve. As Welch noted:

> **We have found that by reaching for what appears to be the impossible, we often actually do the impossible; and even when we don't quite make it, we inevitably wind up doing much better than we would have done.**

In this **self-assessment exercise** you can learn whether you have it within you to aim for stretch goals:

1. Do you feel that you have accomplished all you can once you reach predetermined goals?

       Yes   No

2. Do you feel that you are getting all you can out of your employees?

       Yes   No

3. Do you allow yourself to get into struggles over budgetary figures?

       Yes   No

If you answered yes to all three questions, you need to take a whole new look at notion of setting goals.

STRETCH TARGETS ENERGIZE

Reaching and stretching, argues Welch, is a major breakthrough. It ends all those petty, internal negotiations about budget targets that accomplished little in forging a manager's vision. Budgets enervate. Stretch targets energize.

Welch insists on asking managers and employees to reach for their dreams—and skip the niggling negotiations that are so typical of large companies. Haggling over budget plans is simply an exercise in compromise:

> **People work for a month on charts and presentations and books to come in and tell the CEO that, given the economic environment, given the competitive scenario, the best they can do is Two. Then the CEO says "I have to give the shareholders Four." They eventually settle on Three and everyone goes home happy.**

BULLET TRAIN MENTALITY

In order to illuminate the importance of stretch, Welch points admiringly to the Japanese executive who was thinking stretch when he talked about the "bullet-train mentality." The executive noted that to double the Japanese bullet train's speed, it would be necessary to do far more than merely refine the engine. Every aspect of the infrastructure surrounding the bullet train, including the rails and the overhead cable, would have to be studied and possibly altered. A new paradigm was needed, some monumental improvement. Observed Welch:

> **You've got to think out of the box. It's not the same train with a little more tweak. It's a whole new thought. So all the talks are about big things! Double the speed of the bullet train—don't go ten miles an hour faster. That's what stretch is.**

Dreams Are Exciting; Decimal Points Aren't

In one of his Letters to Share Owners, Welch said this about "stretch":

> **Stretch is a concept that would have produced smirks, if not laughter, in the GE of three or four years ago, because it essentially means using dreams to set business targets—with no real idea of how to get there. If you do know how to get there—it's not a stretch target. We certainly didn't have a clue how we were going to get to ten inventory turns when we set that target. But we're getting there, and as soon as we become sure we can do it, it's time for another stretch.**

That was classic Jack Welch thinking. Never be content with the present. Never let the present dictate your future. Don't be comfortable with the present.

DON'T PUNISH FOR MISSING BIG TARGETS

Arguing over budgetary numbers in conference rooms did not inspire the people on the shop or office floors who had to deliver the numbers. Welch stopped such behavior. He liked to say that in a boundaryless organization, with a bias for speed, decimal points were a bore. They inspired or challenged no one. They captured no imaginations.

What happens if employees fail to reach goals? Welch called this a "crucial issue":

> **If they don't have the team operating effectively, you give them another chance. If they fail again, you hand the reins to another person. But you don't punish for not meeting big targets. If ten is the target and you're only at two, we'll have a party when you go to four. We'll give out bonuses and go out on the town and drink or whatever. When you reach six, we'll celebrate again. We don't waste time and money budgeting 4.12 to 5.13 to 6.17.**

Welch seemed aware of the pitfalls of stretch. Say for example that someone at a lower level worked hard to improve upon the previous year's performance, and at the end of the year succeeded. But that person's boss, striving for a much higher stretch performance target, was disappointed and berated the worker for "only" delivering what he or she deemed to be mediocre results. This made for an unhappy manager and an unmotivated employee.

So, acknowledged Welch, stretch was not an easy concept. It took time to implement successfully, and it depended a great deal on senior managers and junior managers building trust in one another. Welch observed that if an employee had a terrible relationship, where a boss took a stretch goal and stamped it as a plan and then nailed the employee because he or she didn't reach it, the stretch program would be dead:

> **I have no issue with people who work for me who come in with big plans, big dreams, big stuff. They know we're not going to nail them because they didn't make their plan. We're going to nail them because they didn't execute in the context of the environment they're in. Or we're going to reward them for getting close to the plan they wanted in the context of the environment they're in.**

Notice that Jack Welch only began his stretch program in the early 1990s, knowing that it would have been too much to ask for in the painful years of restructuring. Just as he could not expect to empower employees through Work-Out until the major downsizing efforts were concluded, he could not introduce stretch until his leaders were confident that their businesses were performing optimally.

The Jack Welch GE Way Prescription for Encouraging Employees to Stretch Their Goals:

➤ Don't automatically settle for second-best when you can achieve more. Reach for the stars.

➤ You may fail. In fact, you probably will fail. But stretching yourself, and stretching your business, is going to improve performance results.

➤ Be more creative, be more imaginative, be more thoughtful about your business. The more you think about how to get more out of your business, the higher your stretch targets and the better off you're going to be.

P A R T V

DRIVE QUALITY THROUGHOUT THE ORGANIZATION

*You've got to be passionate lunatics
about the quality issue.*

CHAPTER 19

LIVE QUALITY—AND DRIVE COST AND SPEED FOR COMPETITIVE ADVANTAGE

As boundaryless learning has defined how we behave, six sigma quality will ... define how we work.

*I*N THE LATE 1990S, ONE CONCEPT DROVE GENERAL ELECTRIC with unwavering intensity, an intensity that was evident at every GE business throughout the world. And this concept was quality.

Of course, by the late 1990s quality was hardly a new concept. Companies like Motorola had been living quality for years. But when Jack Welch embraced an idea, he did so with his own brand of fiery commitment and customary all-consuming passion. And as history has shown throughout the years, it was this firebrand enthusiasm that helped turn ordinary company programs into GE strategic initiatives powerful enough to transform the company.

Welch was so taken with quality that he was almost smothering it with his attention, mobilizing the entire company in the effort. For he was convinced that quality improvement would be the breakthrough business strategy that would make General Electric the most competitive company on earth. Once again, Welch was trying to stay one step ahead of the pace, changing before it was absolutely necessary to do so.

Why did Welch choose the late 1990s to focus on quality? It was not as if GE had overlooked quality in the past. On the contrary, quality for General Electric had always been important. And GE's durable products had always been widely regarded as high-quality products.

Yet, GE's products and processes had not yet attained *world-class* quality. Other companies had taken on the role of quality leaders. Companies like Motorola, Toyota, Hewlett-Packard, and Texas Instruments had long since been associated with world-class quality. However, Welch could not have cared less that other companies had beaten him to the punch on quality. In fact, he would use the knowledge and experience gleaned from other companies to create an even better, more powerful program. And he was determined to put GE's stamp on the quality effort from start to finish.

FIGHTING AN ASIAN HURRICANE

While GE had the luxury of choosing its market battlegrounds, some companies like Motorola, Texas Instruments, Hewlett-Packard, and Xerox did not. As Welch describes it, those companies were caught "in the eye of the Asian competitive hurricane" and had to deal head-on with the Japanese invasion that struck many American industries. Because their Asian competitors achieved new levels of quality in their products, Motorola and the other American firms had to improve quality levels or close their doors. As a result, after years of exceptional effort, they achieved a quality level that matched or exceeded all of their global competitors.

When GE benchmarked itself with those companies, it became abundantly clear that there was much room for improving the quality of GE's products and processes. "It's gotten better with each succeeding generation of product and service," declared Welch. "But it has not improved enough to get us to the quality levels of that small circle of excellent global companies that had survived the intense competitive assault by themselves, achieving new levels of quality."

Learning from the experience of those American enterprises, Welch decided to make quality a crucial management focus at GE. Quality, to be blunt, had become a Welch obsession.

It was not as if Welch had rejected quality improvement in the past. He had simply assumed—incorrectly, in his judgment—that he could attack the issue of quality by concentrating on other aspects of business: by increasing productivity, and getting employees and suppliers more involved in the company; and by emphasizing the three S's: speed, simplicity, and self-confidence.

SPEED WILL GIVE US QUALITY

Only when Welch discovered that the three S's weren't doing the trick did he become convinced that something else was needed.

GE had launched quality programs in the past, but they weren't taken seriously. They relied on slogans over substance.

For a number of years, Jack Welch had been urging greater levels of productivity from GE personnel. Yet by the mid-1990s, employees argued that greater productivity was impossible without improving the quality of GE's products and processes. Too much time was spent on fixing and reworking a product before it left the factory. That cut down on GE's speed, one of Welch's supreme corporate tenets, and also reduced productivity. GE customers were pleased with GE's quality, but executives discovered much waste in the mending of bad quality before it reached the customer. No one really looked at how much time was being wasted by the failure to produce a high-quality product on the first round and having to rework it extensively before it was ready to be shipped.

Still, the inertia at GE over quality had a longstanding basis. First of all, Welch had made the Work-Out program the focus of General Electric's key strategic initiatives in the late 1980s and early 1990s. It was taken for granted that Work-Out would keep General

Electric's quality high. Then, too, the Crotonville experience—where GE's managers learned how to manage large-scale change—would, it was assumed, lead to high quality levels.

THE ONLY REAL VALUE CHOICE

Welch felt that it wasn't enough to have products and services that were merely equal to and better than those of GE's competitors:

> **We want to be more than that. We want to change the competitive landscape by being not just better than our competitors, but by taking quality to a whole new level. We want to make our quality so special, so valuable to our customers, so important to their success that our products become their only real value choice.**

The question was how to come up with a companywide quality campaign that didn't repeat the mistakes of the prior programs. Welch and his colleagues found the answer in six sigma, the concept that had been pioneered by Motorola, the Illinois-based maker of communications equipment and semiconductors.

Six Sigma

Six sigma is a measurement of mistakes per one million discreet operations. It applies to all transactions, not just manufacturing. The lower the number of errors, the higher the quality. One sigma means that 68 percent of the products are acceptable; three sigma means 99.7 percent are acceptable; six sigma, the ultimate goal, means that 99.999997 percent are acceptable. Six sigma denotes more quality than three sigma: at six sigma, only 3.4 defects per million operations occur. At three and a half sigma, which is an average quality measure for most companies, there are 35,000 defects per million.

High quality has long since been associated with the Japanese. Japanese goods like watches and televisions had for some time met six sigma standards. The quality of American goods, in contrast, was hovering around four sigma. But Japan's high standards of quality applied only to products such as electric equipment, cars, and precision instruments—and only to the area of production. Japan continued to lag behind in the effort to improve quality and productivity by improving business *processes* (as GE would attempt to do through its six sigma quality initiative).

SHOULD GE FOLLOW MOTOROLA?

In the late 1980s and early 1990s, Motorola pioneered the six sigma initiative and in the process reduced the number of defects in its products from four to five and a half sigma, yielding $2.2 billion in savings. Other firms, such as AlliedSignal and Texas Instruments, began to adopt their own six sigma quality programs.

Throughout 1994 and early 1995, Welch and other GE executives began mulling over what to do to improve GE's quality. The chairman was in a quandary. He agreed with others that GE was ripe for a massive effort at quality improvement. But what he first saw of the six sigma approach turned him off. He worried that it was inconsistent with his other business values and strategies:

- It was centrally managed
- It seemed too bureaucratic, with reports and standard nomenclature
- It called for specifically agreed-upon measures

In short, the initiative simply didn't feel like a GE program. Work-Out, on the other hand, felt very much like a GE program: breaking down bureaucratic boundaries, encouraging openness, and urging people to learn from one another.

But ultimately his own employees, especially those in manufacturing and engineering, swayed Welch. They were the first to recognize that the company needed a solid quality initiative. These "hands-on" people understood that after several years of great growth in productivity and inventory turns, progress had faltered because of the high number of defects in its business processes.

In April 1995, a month before Welch was hospitalized for ten days for triple-bypass heart surgery, the company did a survey that showed that GE employees were dissatisfied with the quality of its products and processes. (It should be noted that the results of the survey had nothing to do with the chairman's heart ailments.)

It was increasingly apparent that a number of other companies, including Motorola and Texas Instruments, had achieved dramatic results through six sigma programs.

A Crucial Meeting

Then, in June, the CEO at AlliedSignal, Larry Bossidy, spoke to Welch's Corporate Executive Council. Bossidy was highly regarded at GE. He was a former GE vice chairman and one of Welch's closest friends. In 1994, Bossidy had launched a six sigma program at AlliedSignal. Now, a year later, he told the CEC how impressed he was with it and how he thought GE could benefit enormously from undertaking a similar effort. Welch, who had enormous respect for Bossidy, concluded that if six sigma was good enough for Larry Bossidy, it might be good enough for Jack Welch.

What particularly attracted Welch to six sigma was its heavy reliance on statistics. This quality program would not be "fluffy," a word he had used to describe previous, discredited GE quality efforts. Welch truly hoped that *this* quality program would not sink in a tide of indifference, as previous ones had. "This is not the program of the month," he said. "This is a discipline. This will be forever."

If GE could pull off a successful quality program, the potential rewards were enormous. The cost of remaining at three sigma or four sigma amounted to as much as 10 to 15 percent of a company's revenues. For General Electric, that would translate into a cost of $8 billion to $12 billion.

The Jack Welch GE Way Prescription for Assuring Quality In Your Business:

➤ Don't get hung up over the need for soft values. Some programs have to be centrally managed; some have to depend on specifically agreed measures.

➤ Don't simply assume that your company is doing well at quality.

➤ Once you decide to introduce a quality program, make sure it's companywide.

CHAPTER 20

MAKE QUALITY THE JOB OF
EVERY EMPLOYEE

*By 2000, we want to be not just better in
quality, but a company 10,000 times
better than its competitors.*

JACK WELCH MADE AN OFFICIAL ANNOUNCEMENT
launching the quality initiative at GE's annual gathering of 500 top
managers in January 1996. He called the program "the biggest
opportunity for growth, increased profitability, and individual
employee satisfaction in the history of our company." GE set itself
a goal of becoming a six sigma quality company by the year 2000.
Such a company produces nearly defect-free products, services,
and transactions.

THE TOUGHEST STRETCH GOAL

Welch called six sigma the most difficult stretch goal GE had ever
undertaken. Prior to the quality initiative, GE's typical processes
generated about 35,000 defects per million operations, or three
and a half sigma. While that number of defects may sound astro-
nomical, it was actually consistent with the defect levels of most
successful U.S. enterprises.

By way of comparison, airlines have a safety record that is less than one-half failure per million operations, while their baggage operations are in the 35,000 to 50,000 defect range. This is typical of manufacturing and service operations, as well as the totaling of restaurant bills, payroll processing, and doctors' prescriptions.

To reach six sigma, GE needed to reduce its defect rates by 10,000. To achieve this level of performance by 2000, it would have to reduce defect levels an average of 84 percent a year! Welch observed that

> **Six sigma—GE Quality 2000—will be the biggest, the most personally rewarding, and, in the end, the most profitable undertaking in our history.**

Motorola took ten years to reach six sigma. Welch hoped to do it in five years. Was that possible?

The GE chairman felt his goal was realistic. Motorola, after all, had to pioneer the program. It had to develop the tools. GE had the advantage of coming along later. And it benefited from the Work-Out culture, which enabled its employees to be more responsive to a quality initiative. Welch was confident that GE would do rapidly what other companies took much longer to accomplish.

THE NEW WARRIOR CLASS

The six sigma program relied upon an entire new "warrior class" within the company to carry out its aims and procedures. This warrior class consisted of:

- Green belts
- Black belts
- Master black belts

The various "belts" represented managers who had undergone complex statistical training in six sigma.

On July 19, 1997, Welch sent a letter, written in longhand, to all Corporate Executive Council attendees, describing what he felt should be the five characteristics of the people who steer the quality program through its rigors:

1. Enormous energy and passion for the job—a real leader; sees it operationally, not as a "staffer."
2. Ability to excite, energize, and mobilize organization around six sigma benefits—not a bureaucrat.
3. Understands six sigma is all about customers winning in their marketplace and GE bottom line.
4. Has technical grasp of six sigma, which is equal to or bettered by strong financial background and capability.
5. Has a real edge to deliver bottom-line results and not just technical solutions.

From Billing a Customer to Making a Lightbulb

Initially GE was concentrating on cutting out wasteful expenditures of time and effort. The focus was on such disparate elements as:

- Billing a customer
- Making the base of an incandescent light bulb
- Approving a credit card application
- Installing a turbine
- Lending money
- Servicing an aircraft engine
- Answering a service call for an appliance
- Underwriting an insurance policy
- Developing software for a new CAT product
- Overhauling a locomotive
- Invoicing an industrial distributor

In its first year or so, employees considered six sigma just another new management fad, and word of the program filtered throughout the company slowly. This was not what GE's organizers had in mind. So Welch applied his fiery zeal to promoting the program personally. He talked it up in speeches every chance he got and even distributed a pamphlet about it (*The Goal and the Journey*) in the spring of 1996.

At the GE operating managers' meeting in January 1997, the chairman made a startling declaration: He proclaimed that GE's managers would have to get "on board" the quality initiative—or face dismissal!

> **Simply put, quality must be the central activity of every person in this room. You can't be balanced about this subject. You've got to be lunatics about this subject. You've got to be passionate lunatics about the quality issue. You've got to be out on the fringe of demand and pressure and push to make this happen. This has to be central to everything you do every day . . . Every one of you here is a quality champion or you shouldn't be here.**

Welch insisted that employees at every level of the company live six sigma. Six sigma would have to become the common language of General Electric.

NO BELT, NO PROMOTION

In his Letter to Share Owners in 1996, Welch reminded his staff of the penalty some would pay for not heeding his decree to take six sigma seriously:

> **The methodologies of six sigma we learned from other companies, but the cultural obsessiveness and all-encompassing passion for it is pure GE. For leaders who do not see how critical quality is to our future—like leaders who could not become boundaryless during the 1980s—GE is simply not the place to be.**

If these messages weren't enough, Welch dropped one more none-too-subtle hint in March 1997, when he sent a fax to managers around the world clarifying promotion requirements associated with six sigma quality. In it he wrote that effective January 1, 1998, one must have started green belt or black belt training in order to be promoted to a senior middle management or senior management position. And effective January 1, 1999, all of GE's "professional" employees, numbering between 80,000 and 90,000 and including officers, must have begun green belt or black belt training.

Welch's message was a clear threat: If you don't have a belt, you won't get promoted. "We've got to say only people that have black belt training will lead businesses in this company in the next century." To drive the point home, he tied an astounding 40 percent of his 120 vice presidents' bonuses to progress toward quality results.

As boundaryless learning defined how GE employees behave, six sigma quality would, Welch contended, define how GE employee teams worked. In a speech given at an annual meeting in April 1997, he again took a tough stance:

> **In the next century we will neither accept nor keep anyone without a quality mind set, a quality focus. It has been remarked that we are just a bit "unbalanced" on the subject. That's a fair comment. We are.**

After Welch's repeated warnings that GE staffers had to "volunteer" for six sigma, it was hardly surprising that the number of applicants for training programs rose dramatically. One could feel the excitement the program was generating during a visit to various GE installations in the summer of 1997. It all seemed like a boot camp with the sole purpose of "rallying the troops" behind the quality program. To say the least, GE employees had become obsessive about the program!

GOING TO WAR?

Welch knew he had set some pretty tough stretch targets in the quality initiative, but he had no qualms at all. In the summer of

1997 a journalist told Welch that a former GE manager had equated working for Welch with going to war: Many people die, and the survivors are left to face the next battle. The CEO responded somewhat angrily:

> **Does this look like a war? I really don't think that's appropriate. On the other hand, I cannot achieve my objectives if I say to my people, "I think the quality's great and I'd like you to think so too." I have to say to my managers, "Forty percent of your bonus depends on how few faults your groups are responsible for." I have to tell them that anyone who wants to be working here in two years' time must undergo the training.**

A reporter asked Welch what he would say to a GE factory employee who asked, "What's in the quality program for me? "

Welch replied: "Job security. Enhanced satisfaction. Not wasteful rework. Growth."

But wouldn't the GE employee work eight hours on the factory floor whether there was a quality program or not?

Sure, was the thrust of Welch's answer, but without six sigma the employee's job might become tenuous. With six sigma, a quality program that focuses on customers' needs, the employee had a better chance that his or her job would be needed in the future.

Had Welch gotten his way, six sigma would have spread throughout GE like lightning, improving products and processes overnight. But GE was far too big for that to happen, filled with too many people who had been doing their jobs for too many years to adopt major changes that quickly. Welch, however, still believed in speed and self-confidence as effective business strategies, and he wanted self-confident GE personnel to inculcate six sigma into their jobs quickly. By April 1997, Welch remarked in a speech—less than two years into the program—"six sigma has gone from being an alien concept, full of complex calculations and unfamiliar jargon, to a consuming passion sweeping across the company."

The Jack Welch GE Way Prescription for Taking a Company to Six Sigma Standards:

➤ Develop a technical knowledge of six sigma so that it becomes second nature to you.

➤ Put all your energy and passion into creating six sigma conditions.

➤ Keep in sight that six sigma concentrates on customers, not just reaching certain numbers.

CHAPTER 21

TO ACHIEVE QUALITY: MEASURE, ANALYZE, IMPROVE, AND CONTROL

Quality is the next act of productivity.

*T*HE SIX SIGMA APPROACH TO QUALITY IMPROVEMENT in business processes entails the formation of project teams, each aimed at achieving the six sigma level of precision through a four-step process known as MAIC:

- Measurement
- Analysis
- Improvement
- Control

Essentially, these steps call for probing, measuring, and analyzing in order to discover the root causes of the problem—and then controlling those causes to keep the problem from recurring. The control phase is crucial. In the past at GE things got fixed, but they didn't *stay* fixed because there were few real controls. For the first time, the six sigma approach addressed this issue. GE makes a point of auditing its quality initiative projects for six to twelve months to assure that the high level of quality remains; the project is then audited every six months thereafter.

HOW SIX SIGMA WORKS

Here is how the six sigma process works at General Electric. First, a project is identified. Then, critical-to-quality characteristics (CTQs) are defined. And finally, the six sigma process begins. Master black belts mentor black belts through the four MAIC steps:

1. *Measure:* Identify the key internal process that influences CTQs and measure the defects generated relative to identified CTQs. Defects are defined as out-of-tolerance CTQs. The end of this phase occurs when the black belt can successfully measure the defects generated for a key process affecting the CTQ.

2. *Analyze:* The objective of this phase is to start to understand why defects are generated. Brainstorming, statistical tools, and so forth are used to identify key variables that cause defects. The output of this phase is the explanation of the variables most likely to drive process variation.

3. *Improve:* Here the objective is to confirm the key variables and then quantify their effect on the CTQs, identify the maximum acceptable ranges of the key variables, make certain the measurement systems are capable of measuring the variation in the key variables, and modify the process to stay within the acceptable ranges.

4. *Control:* The objective of this final phase is to ensure that the modified process now enables the key variables to stay within the maximum acceptable ranges using tools such as statistical process control (SPC) or simple checklists.

Each phase takes one month, beginning with three days of training followed by three weeks of "doing" and a day of formal review by the master black belts and champions. After a black belt finishes the first project under the aegis of a master black belt, he takes on added projects, which are reviewed only by a master black belt. Both master black belts and black belts are expected to work full time in their roles for at least two years.

Black Belts and Green Belts

GE identifies the various players in the six sigma effort as follows:

1. *Champions:* These senior managers define the projects and are responsible for the success of the six sigma efforts. They approve, fund, and troubleshoot. Some business leaders are champions, although most champions report directly to business leaders. A GE business typically will have seven to ten champions. Champions do not have to work full time in the quality program, but they are expected to give as much time as needed to assure the program's success. Champions are trained for one week.

2. *Master black belts:* These are full-time teachers with heavy quantitative skills and tutoring and leadership ability. They are certified upon fulfilling two requirements: They must oversee at least ten black belts who become certified, and they must be approved by the business champion team. They review and mentor black belts. Selection criteria for master black belts are quantitative skills and the ability to teach and mentor. Master black belts are trained for at least two weeks to teach and mentor.

3. *Black belts:* These are full-time quality executives who lead teams and focus on key processes, reporting results back to the champions. These team leaders are responsible for measuring, analyzing, improving, and controlling key processes that influence customer satisfaction or productivity growth. They are certified upon successfully completing two projects: the first under the aegis of a master black belt, the second more autonomously. A successful project is one in which defects are reduced ten times if the process began at less than three sigma (66,000 defects per million operations), or by 50 percent if the process started at greater than three sigma. To become certified, black belts must also be approved by the business champion team.

4. *Green belts:* They work on black belt projects but not full time; they work on six sigma projects while holding down

other jobs in the company. Once the black belt project has ended, team members are expected to continue to use six sigma tools as part of their regular job.

GE planned to train each of its 20,000 engineers so that all new products would be designed for six sigma production. It also planned to train all 270,000 GE employees in six sigma methodology. The goal was for every one of GE's 80,000 to 90,000 professional employees to be green belts.

MEASURING PROGRESS

GE designed five corporate measures to help a business track progress in the six sigma program:

1. *Customer satisfaction:* Each business surveys its customers, asking them to grade GE and the best-in-category on critical-to-quality issues. The grade is a 5-point scale, where 5 is the best and 1 is the worst. A defect is defined as either less than best in a category or a score of 3 or less. GE measures defects per million survey responses. As with all measures in the project, the results are reported on a quarterly basis.

2. *Cost of poor quality:* There are three components: appraisal, which is mostly inspection; internal costs, largely scrap and rework; and external costs, largely warranties and concessions. GE tracks the total as a percent of revenues on a quarterly basis.

3. *Supplier quality:* GE tracks defects per million units purchased, where the defective part has either one or more CTQs out of tolerance and therefore must be returned or reworked, or the part is received outside the schedule.

4. *Internal performance:* GE measures the defects generated by its processes. The measure is the sum of all defects in relation to the sum of all opportunities for defects (CTQs).

5. *Design for manufacturability:* GE measures the percent of drawings reviewed for CTQs and the percent of CTQs designed to six sigma. Most new products are now designed with CTQs identified. GE hopes to begin designing products and services to six sigma capability. This measure is very important, since the design approach often drives the defect levels.

The Snowball Is Growing

Since the six sigma initiative began in October 1995, the results have been nothing less than stunning—exceeding even Jack Welch's lofty expectations.

GE launched its quality initiative in late 1995 with 200 projects and massive training. In 1996, it completed 3,000 projects, each averaging seven months, and trained 30,000 employees. It invested $200 million in the initiative and got a return of nearly that much ($170 million) in quality-related savings.

Welch's six sigma effort was backed by far more resources than any past quality initiative. GE spent $300 million in 1997 and enjoyed a $600 million benefit—so its net benefit was $300 million for the year. At first, it planned to undertake 6,000 projects, but that number grew to 11,000. The average project is five months in length and yields an 80 percent reduction in defects, generating $70,000 to $100,000 in savings.

MEANWHILE, AROUND THE COMPANY

Around GE the results from six sigma were impressive. GE Lighting had a billing system that worked fine but contained one problem: It didn't mesh very well electronically with the purchasing system of Wal-Mart, one of GE's best customers. This caused disputes and delayed payments, and it was a waste of time for Wal-Mart.

Then a GE black belt team used six sigma methodology, information technology, and a $30,000 investment to solve the problem from Wal-Mart's perspective. In four months, defects were reduced by 98 percent. Wal-Mart achieved higher productivity and competitiveness, and fewer disputes and delays resulted.

At GE's Capital Mortgage Corporation, employees fielded some 300,000 telephone calls a year from customers, using voice-mail and callbacks when an employee was not available. To GE, the system seemed satisfactory, since all calls were answered, but there was one major problem: By the time a GE employee returned a particular customer's call, that customer was often talking to another company—the result being lost opportunities and lost sales. Now that was a problem!

A master black belt team was assigned the task of solving this daunting problem. The team learned that one of the corporation's forty-two branches had no such problem; nearly all calls were answered the first time around. Why was that? Analyzing its system, along with process flow, equipment, and physical layout and staffing, the team found the answer and then adapted it to the other forty-one branches. Customers who had found the Mortgage Corporation employees inaccessible nearly 24 percent of the time now had a 99 percent chance of speaking to a GE representative on the very first try; and since 40 percent of their calls resulted in business, the return for GE amounted to millions of dollars.

On a Thursday in March 1996, the chairman got in touch with all GE officers, asking them to provide him with written documentation that would help him decide how large their bonuses would be. In essence, Welch was asking the managers to justify their bonuses by demonstrating the strides they were making in the quality program. He let it be known that 40 percent of their bonuses would be based on their work in this area. The chairman gave them until the following Monday to hand in their responses.

He was disappointed by the results. Some officers at Plastics had made the error of replying vaguely that they planned to train as many black belts as possible. But Welch wanted specifics. *How many?* Some said, with equal vagueness, that they expected benefits to flow from the quality program. The chairman again decried the lack of specifics: *How large would the benefits be?*

By Tuesday an exasperated Welch fired back notes to the officers. "This isn't even close," he told them. He demanded more aggressive commitments from his executives. The chairman's stinging retort got the managers' attention.

Welch had great hopes, dreams, and plans for the quality program. While he had liked its early progress, he knew much work had yet to be done. At first, GE concentrated on improving business processes—with excellent results. Welch next turned his efforts—and the vast resources of GE—to improving the quality of GE's products. He wanted to incorporate six sigma thinking and standards into every new GE product. He knew the company would save time, money, and effort. Even though GE had made remarkable progress in the first two years of the program, Welch still believed six sigma was in its infancy.

The Jack Welch GE Way Prescription for Measuring and Monitoring Six Sigma:

➤ *Measure:* Identify the key internal process that influences CTQs and measure the defects generated relative to identified CTQs.

➤ *Analyze:* Understand why defects are generated.

➤ *Improve:* Confirm the key variables and quantify their effect on the CTQs.

➤ *Control:* Ensure that the modified process enabled the key variables to stay within the maximum acceptable ranges.

THE TOUGHEST BOSS/
MOST ADMIRED
MANAGER IN AMERICA

I don't get involved in pricing. I'm more of a coach.

22

C H A P T E R

JACK WELCH DEALS WITH ADVERSITY

We have no police force, no jails. We must rely on the integrity of our people as our first defense.

*I*T IS NO ACCIDENT that "integrity" was among the first words to appear in General Electric's official version of its corporate values during Jack Welch's era. Unfortunately for both, ethical lapses among GE employees constituted one of the chairman's most perplexing and difficult challenges.

Welch was well aware that breaches had occurred far too often—and he conceded that they would probably occur in the future. For all of GE's bottom-line success (some say *because* of that success), few other major American firms suffered through as many ethical lapses as GE.

NO EXCUSES

Yet Welch never tried to defend or offer excuses, although he did suggest that in any community the size of GE, such violations were unavoidable. After all, he noted, all communities of GE's size had a police force for the simple reason that it was necessary. No one had yet figured out how to eradicate crime completely.

Given the amount of scandal at GE, one might be left wondering how Welch remained unscathed. Why hadn't the controversy, which often adorned the front pages of countless newspapers, including *The Wall Street Journal,* hurt Welch's standing as the nation's most admired CEO?

By this time, the answer should shock no one: Whenever scandal surfaced, he applied his vintage no-nonsense, no-time-to-lose management style to quell the problem. Welch's response took on a certain pattern. First, he moved quickly to rid GE of the transgressors. Next, he made it crystal clear that future transgressors would automatically be dismissed. And last, he made sure everyone knew he personally had nothing to do with the integrity violation in question.

If such ethical lapses occurred at other firms, the CEO would certainly be in hot water and probably in distinct jeopardy of losing his or her job. Yet not once had anyone suggested that Jack Welch should step down as a result of a GE scandal. It was testament to his business acumen (and perhaps his communications staff) that he had always managed to avoid the fray, leaving his golden-boy image intact. Although it might not fit the usual management paradigm as neatly as "face reality" or "fix, close, or sell," surely one of Welch's gifts was his unswerving ability to remain aloof from the company's ethical troubles. It was not a leadership secret one proudly boasted about, but it was part of Welch's business intelligence nonetheless. And there were valuable lessons to be gleaned from how GE's chairman dealt with the company's integrity troubles. Here, then, is a brief look at some of those troubles and how Welch coped with them.

TROUBLE WITH TIME CARDS

On March 26, 1985, nearly four years after he took over as Chairman and CEO of General Electric, the company suffered one of the worst blows of his tenure. On that fateful day, GE was indicted by a federal grand jury on two sets of charges: one set contended that GE's aerospace business had filed $800,000 in incorrect costs on employee time cards; the second set contended that GE had lied to the government about work it had carried out on a nuclear warhead system. GE's work on the nuclear warhead system was the result of a $40.9 million contract that the U.S. Air Force had awarded the company to overhaul fuses on intercontinental ballistic missiles.

Three days after the indictment, Welch, hoping to put the front-page scandal into some perspective, wrote a letter that was distributed to every General Electric employee. He noted that 100 of the 108 counts of the indictment related to 100 time cards, which represented a relatively small portion of the 100,000 time cards filed during that period. "While it is entirely possible," he wrote, "that, during the course of performing several multimillion-dollar contracts, charging errors did occur, there was no criminal wrongdoing on the part of the Company or its employees. The Company has not been convicted of any crime." When other misdeeds occurred in future years, the CEO would use the same argument quite effectively—that the transgression was the act of a few rotten apples and that the company overall was not involved.

As Welch observed after the aerospace indictments, "In any large organization—and GE with its 330,000 total employees is a very large organization—people may make errors in judgment. These must be viewed in relation to the extremely good reputation of our company and its people." After a low-level employee confessed, GE pleaded guilty to the aerospace charges and was fined $1.04 million.

Other infractions followed:

- In 1989, GE settled four civil suits that were brought by whistle-blowers who had alleged that General Electric had cheated the government of millions of dollars by issuing faulty time cards. GE paid $3.5 million.

- In 1990, GE was convicted of defrauding the Defense Department as a result of overcharging the U.S. Army for a battlefield computer system. GE paid $30 million in penalties for that infraction and other defense contracting overcharges.

■ In 1992, GE pleaded guilty to defrauding the Pentagon out of more than $30 million in the sale of military jet engines to Israel when an employee took bribes. GE paid $69 million in fines.

■ In 1993, GE's NBC News unit staged a misleading simulated crash test, which led to the unit's on-air apology to General Motors. NBC also agreed to pay GM an estimated $1 million in legal and investigation expenses.

■ In 1994, in one of the most embarrassing and most widely publicized scandals of that year, head government T-bond trader Joseph Jett of Kidder Peabody (GE's brokerage unit) concocted $350 million in phony profits over a twenty-nine-month period before being fired in April of that year. As a result, GE was forced to take a $210 million charge against its first-quarter earnings in 1994.

The pertinent question posed by the press—and perhaps by folks at countless water coolers across the country—was this: Was Welch personally responsible for these incidents? *Fortune* magazine certainly thought so: "Most troubling is that [Joseph] Jett's misdeeds, if true, are not an isolated case at GE. When you put the Kidder scandal together with other transgressions that have sullied GE's reputation over the past decade . . . you begin to get a sense that somewhere in the highly successful and celebrated GE culture something is not right." The corollary to the magazine's claim was that, in putting great pressure on his managers to perform, Welch encouraged them to look after their self-interests at the expense of company loyalty. Put another way, if you encourage the winning-is-everything mentality, don't hide your head in the sand when trouble hits the fan.

What Can One Do?

To Welch's chagrin, other than take a tough stand against transgressors, he discovered there was precious little a CEO could do *in advance* to ward off such integrity lapses. One step he did take in 1987 was to issue companywide guidelines, an 80-page booklet called *Integrity: The Spirit and the Letter of Our Commitment.* Every new employee was required to read the booklet and sign a card found in the booklet (or answer by e-mail) that they had read it. And all other employees had to do the same once a year. In that booklet, Welch wrote in his Statement of Integrity:

> **Integrity is the rock upon which we build our business success—and our quality products and services, our forthright relations with customers and suppliers, and ultimately, our winning competitive record. GE's quest for competitive excellence begins and ends with our commitments to ethical conduct.**

He then urged all employees to make a personal commitment to follow GE's code of conduct, to obey applicable laws and regulations, to avoid all conflicts of interest, to be honest, fair, and trustworthy.

THE JACK WELCH DEFENSE

Welch testified before the Subcommittee on Oversight and Investigations of the House Committee on Energy and Commerce in Washington, D.C., on July 29, 1992. He refused to make excuses for GE's misdeeds: "Theft of a dollar is theft and fraud is fraud," he told the committee. He also refuted the notion that his aggressive management style led to the integrity violations. There was a view, he noted, that an atmosphere where excellence and performance are always in demand is an atmosphere that encourages breaking the rules.

> **What's the solution? Tell athletes to run slower, jump lower, so they'll be above suspicion? Our view, put in those terms, is that you must run as fast as you can, and jump as high as you can, but if you break the rules, your medals are gone and you're out of the game for good.**

Welch went on to point out that there are no second chances for those who violate the ethical code:

> No one at GE loses a job because of a missed quar-
> ter . . . a missed year . . . or a mistake. That's nonsense and
> everyone knows it. A company would be paralyzed in an
> atmosphere like that. People get second chances. Many
> get thirds and fourths, along with training, help, even dif-
> ferent jobs. There is only one performance failure where
> there is no second chance. That's a clear integrity viola-
> tion. If you commit one of those, you're out . . .

One Violation, and You're Out

In December 1997, in an interview with the author, Welch talked at
length about his handling of the integrity issue at GE. He began by
recalling an internal GE meeting he had recently attended at which
an NBC intern asked him if he could guarantee that GE would never
have a "Texaco incident." (The intern was referring to the 1996 incident in which Texaco officials were caught on tape making racist re-
marks; the officials had to pay $115 million in reparations.) Welch
said no, he couldn't make such an ironclad guarantee:

> I can't guarantee anyone in this room that you're not a
> thief. That you haven't stolen something. Or robbed some-
> body this morning. All I know is that if I knew that, you
> wouldn't be on the payroll. We have a code of conduct
> here that anybody we know who's doing something won't
> be on this payroll for an hour.

When asked how he had managed to cope with GE's scandals
and remain unscathed, he replied:

> Look, that would be the most overstatement one could
> have, that I've figured out how to deal with this. I've fig-
> ured out one thing: I figured out that I cannot personally
> police perfect behavior of this organization. I can, though,
> have a set of values. Integrity. We have talked about it at
> every meeting. A violation of integrity. There's no discus-
> sion. You are gone. And we have example after example
> where people are just taken right out the door.

Perhaps the real reason Welch has gone unscathed over the
years has to do with the subject Welch hated to talk about—the

numbers. The fact was that GE's numbers—its revenues and earnings—were nothing short of remarkable and were rarely affected by the scandals. Since no harm had come to the company, there had been little motivation for anyone to hold the chairman's feet to the fire. In addition, Welch had persuaded everyone—justifiably—that he was above the fray, that he had not been personally involved with any of the ethical lapses that had plagued GE.

The Jack Welch GE Way Prescription for Achieving Integrity:

➤ If you're running a company, particularly a large one, some sort of ethical breach is probably inevitable.

➤ In order to keep matters from getting out of hand, deal with the problem head on: fire the violator.

➤ Then let others know that any similar breach will be treated the same way.

➤ If you are not personally involved, let the world know that immediately.

CHAPTER 23

JACK WELCH DEALS WITH
THE NEXT GENERATION

*The ability to energize is the
ingredient that counts.*

JACK WELCH LOVED CROTONVILLE, the Leadership
Development Center, a 50-acre campus nestled in the Hudson
Valley of New York that is the brainstorming center for GE's senior
managers and a center of education for junior managers. He loved
its openness, the confrontational style of debate, and most of all the
glimpse it gave him into what was really going on inside GE.
Crotonville provided Welch with the perfect forum for imparting
his business insights to large numbers of employees. So it was no
surprise that he visited its training nucleus some twelve times a year.

On one September day, Welch spoke for three hours to a group of
seventy senior executives who had been identified as "high pots," can-
didates with high potential for even bigger jobs at GE. They were attending a three-week course in manager development where they
would acquire skills that would enable them to run one of GE's businesses. According to the syllabus, "Participants develop executive
skills in relation to key business issues, such as developing business
strategy, competing globally, diversity and globalization, leading
teams and change, and advancing customer satisfaction."

Welch walked briskly into the main auditorium. With its five horseshoe-shaped rows stacked one on top of the other, it has been carefully designed to evoke a certain mood. GE personnel had dubbed the room "The Pit" to indicate that whoever stands in front of an audience here is likely to face tough questioning.

But did that include Jack Welch?

The audience—mid-level executives with GE for roughly ten years, one-quarter of them women, nearly half non-Americans—was a key target group for Welch. Conveying his message to senior executives had been a far easier task than getting the word out to junior-level managers. He was there to tell the audience what leadership is all about. No other subject in business was closer to Welch's heart. He had given much thought to the concept of leadership for decades. He also had the chance to put many of his leadership ideas to the test, and the bottom-line results were remarkable. The public's reaction to Welch and his leadership had been extraordinary. He was routinely described as one of the country's most powerful and impressive leaders. So the GE chairman believed, quite correctly, that he had something meaningful to say about what makes a good business leader—and what does not.

Welch did not like to dwell on numbers; he preferred to talk values. If the company got the values right, the numbers would follow. He was there not just to teach leadership, but also to turn the audience into better GE leaders. A business leader, he suggested, had to be able to make solid judgments about personnel. Welch told the audience

> **My whole job is people. I can't design an engine. I have to bet on people. I'm not like Andy Grove at Intel. He knows how to make a chip. I know I couldn't add anything to a refrigerator. The CEOs of car companies are car guys, so they do product reviews . . . I don't get involved in appliances, plastics pricing. I'm more of a coach. I'll get involved in acquisitions a great deal, and people.**

Welch then remarked that he was proud so many in the company (27,000 in early 1998) were receiving stock options. The GE executive who owned stock options was more likely to care about the company as a whole, since his or her financial future was linked directly to the company's financial future. He openly admitted that stock options were one of his greatest "weapons": by distributing them selectively to certain managers and leaders, he could be sure that his ideas would be carried out. He did not believe in handing out options as if they were Christmas candy. He much preferred giving them to those who were helping to advance his favorite management initiative, the companywide quality program.

KEEP THE A'S, NURTURE THE B'S, DISCARD THE C'S

Welch then worked with the class to define the characteristics of a great business leader.

> **The most important job you have is "growing" your people, giving them a chance to reach their dreams. Your problem is that you won't face the decision to get A's around you all the time.**

Welch divides leaders into A's, B's, and C's: the A's he keeps; the B's he nurtures; the C's he dismisses.

Welch said that a leader must have a vision and be able to articulate that vision, drive its implementation throughout the organization. Being able to articulate the vision "is where energy comes in. You cannot say your vision enough times. You have to bore yourself silly." Many managers do everything but drive the implementation.

> **This is where the edge comes in. Edge is all about making a decision. You may have had a great vision, but you need the courage to have the edge . . . If people have the right values, you give them a second chance. This is a numbers culture. That's the stamp of approval. That gets you another look. This is a performance-driven culture. The great leader without managerial skills runs into trouble. A lot of it is in recycling. There is nothing worse than a manager who sits on his butt counting nickels and dimes and catching people doing things . . . You don't say "I hope to do this." You *do* things. You *make it happen.* It's becoming clear that the ability to energize is the ingredient that counts.**

What did we learn from this day with Professor Welch? It was clear that he regarded honest, open, even confrontational debate as an essential ingredient of every good organization. He also believed that employees closest to the businesses—and closest to the customers—can teach the leaders a great deal. One fact was abundantly clear: Jack Welch and GE placed a great deal of value on training, and backed up that commitment by investing heavily in that vital function.

The Jack Welch GE Way Prescription for Training New Managers:

➤ If you're a manager in an organization, think about the last time your company sent you or a colleague away for three straight weeks of training.

➤ If you are the leader of an organization, think about what your company can do to better train and inculcate the values of the company into the hearts and minds of your troops. You do not need a lavish, three-week affair to inject a bit of the GE Way into your organization!

➤ In fact, you may want to start off smaller and simpler, with some honest-to-goodness open dialogue.

INDEX